W9-BOP-010

Words That Built a Nation

A Young Person's Collection of Historic American Documents

Marilyn Miller

A Stonesong Press Book

SCHOLASTIC INC.
New York Toronto London Auckland Sydney
Mexico City New Delhi Hong Kong

Designed by Michaelis/Carpelis Design Associates, Inc.

Photo Credits:
Every effort has been made to determine and credit the rightful copyright owner of all photos and illustrations contained herein:
Agence France Presse/Corbis-Bettmann: 162, 167; American Antiquarian Society:10; American Heritage Picture Collection: 87; AP/Wide World Photos: 120, 153; Black Star: 143, 145; Sally Anderson Bruce—Museum of American Political Life: 147; Chicago Historical Society: 90; Concord Free Public Library: 13; Corbis: 6 (bottom), 7; Corbis-Bettmann: 4-5 (bottom), 6 (top), 9, 12, 16 (bottom), 35, 38, 64, 75, 77, 80, 82, 84, 102, 129, 166; The Granger Collection: 39, 63, 81; John F. Kennedy Library: 116, 119, 131; Library of Congress: 5 (top), 8, 14, 16 (top)-18, 20, 22, 24, 29, 33, 40, 44-45, 50-51, 52, 54-56, 66 (bottom), 69-70, 73-74, 76, 94-96, 101, 105-106, 128, 138, 144; The Metropolitan Museum of Art, Gift of I.N. Phelps Stokes, Edward S. Hawes, Alice Mary Hawes, Marion Augusta Hawes, 1937: 66 (top); Museum of the City of New York: 91; NASA: 148; National Archives: 25, 27, 41, 59, 72, 78, 92-93, 98, 100, 108, 110, 132 (left), 134; National Park Service, Ellis Island Immigration Museum: 103-104; The New York Public Library Picture Collection: 60; Ronald Reagan Library: 156-157, 161; Franklin Delano Roosevelt Library: 109; University of Illinois at Chicago, The University Library, Jane Addams Memorial Collection: 88; UPI/Corbis-Bettman: 86-87, 112-114, 123-124, 127, 132 (right), 137, 140, 150, 154-155, 162

Copyright © 1999 by The Stonesong Press, Inc., and Marilyn Miller
All rights reserved. Published by Scholastic Inc.
SCHOLASTIC and associated logos are trademarks and/or registered trademarks of Scholastic Inc.

No part of this publication may be reproduced in whole or in part, or stored in a retrieval system, or transmitted in any form or by any means, electronic, mechanical, photocopying, recording, or otherwise, without written permission of the publisher.
For information regarding permission, write to Scholastic Inc., Attention:
Permissions Department, 555 Broadway, New York, NY 10012.

ISBN 0-590-30146-2

Copyright © 1999 by The Stonesong Press, Inc., and Marilyn Miller. All rights reserved.
Published by Scholastic Inc. SCHOLASTIC and associated logos are trademarks and/or registered trademarks of Scholastic Inc.

12 11 10 9 8 7 6 5 4 3 2 3 4 5/0

Printed in the U.S.A. 40

First Scholastic paperback printing, January 2000

Contents

Introduction 1

The Mayflower Compact 4
Poor Richard's Almanack, Benjamin Franklin 6
Speech to the Second Virginia Convention,
Patrick Henry 8
Common Sense, Thomas Paine 12
Letter to John Adams, Abigail Adams 16
The Declaration of Independence 18
The Constitution and The Bill of Rights 24
Farewell Address, George Washington 44
The Star-Spangled Banner, Francis Scott Key 52
The Monroe Doctrine, James Monroe 56
Declaration of Sentiments, Seneca Falls
Convention 60
Uncle Tom's Cabin, Harriet Beecher Stowe 66
The Emancipation Proclamation,
Abraham Lincoln 70
The Gettysburg Address, Abraham Lincoln 74
The Fourteenth Amendment 76
The Fifteenth Amendment 80
I Will Fight No More Forever, Chief Joseph 82
Statement on the Causes of Wounded Knee,
Red Cloud 84
Twenty Years at Hull-House, Jane Addams 88

The Sixteenth Amendment 92
The Fourteen Points, Woodrow Wilson 94
The Nineteenth Amendment 100
The Immigration Act 102
War Message to Congress,
Franklin Delano Roosevelt 106
Brown v. *Board of Education of Topeka* 110
Inaugural Address, John F. Kennedy 114
The Declaration of Indian Purpose 120
Silent Spring, Rachel Carson 124
Speech at the Berlin Wall, John F. Kennedy 128
The March on Washington Address,
Martin Luther King, Jr. 132
The Ballot or The Bullet, Malcolm X 138
Speech to Striking Grape Workers, César Chávez 144
The Eagle Has Landed 148
I'd Rather Be Black Than Female,
Shirley Chisholm 150
Letter of Resignation, Richard M. Nixon 154
Farewell Address, Ronald Reagan 156
Speech at the United Nations Conference on Women,
Hillary Rodham Clinton 162

Afterword 169

Index 170

INTRODUCTION

Even as a young boy, Paul Revere was an organizer. Yes, the man who warned his countrymen of the British mobilization that started the Revolutionary War, found his voice early on. Eager to get involved in ringing the bells at their church, Paul Revere and his friends formed the Bell Ringers Association. They designed a document that stated their goals, and one by one they signed their names to the paper that would govern their organization. What is remarkable about this, however, is not that Revere's career as an organizer began when he was thirteen years old. Rather, it is that he helped create a document that outlined a plan.

War defines boundaries, but it is the treaties that enforce them. Politicians win votes, but it is their speeches and laws that effect change. And activism unites people with slogans and marches, but it is the documents that record struggle, and the proposals for change that promote civil progress. Indeed, while the actions of people defend, define, and rally for their country's success, it is their words that build a nation.

Words capture the battles, the crises, and the politics of a developing government. They are the living history of a country. And the words compiled in this book represent the past, present, and future of ours. They come from speeches, pamphlets, letters, declarations, and songs. They are the bricks and mortar of the United States of America.

In 1621 the European settlers who came to North America brought with them wishes for freedom and fears of failure. The Mayflower passengers knew that if they were to succeed, they would need a governing document. Before they even touched land, they developed the compact that began the spat of trials and errors that turned settlements into colonies, colonies into states, and states into a nation.

The Mayflower Compact and other living documents connect our past to our present. Generations of Americans since then have developed, interpreted, and applied the concepts in these documents to changing events and social conditions. From the Declaration of Independence (1776), to the Declaration of Sentiments (1848), to the Declaration of Indian Purpose (1961), this country's sense of government and freedom runs through its veins and finds its expression in print.

Besides these cornerstone documents, many of the other documents chosen represent turning points in American history. Their existence altered the course, or direction, of the nation by influencing popular opinion. Afterward, the country and the people were forever changed. This was true of Harriet Beecher Stowe's novel *Uncle Tom's Cabin*, which informed a still-skeptical society of the horrors of slavery. And the same is true for President Nixon's one-sentence letter of resignation, which forever altered the way we look at the office of the President of the United States of America.

Some of the documents included here expanded the nation by letting more voices be heard in our society. In 1870 the Fifteenth Amendment secured the vote for African-American men. Fifty years later, in 1920, the approval of the Nineteenth Amendment gave women the same right.

The nation's expansion took economic forms as well. Although it began as a nation of farmers, the United States ultimately became a great industrial power as well. This rise brought both promise and problems. By the end of the nineteenth century, waves of immigrants searching for jobs entered the United States in greater numbers than before. Most of the newcomers settled in cities, where they added to the richness and diversity of American life. Included in this collection is a 1910 account by reformer Jane Addams of the poor conditions immigrants had to face. Indeed, many reformers tried to include newcomers in American life, but others resented them. Prejudice against minorities was widespread and many Americans were concerned that immigrants would take their jobs away.

In the later half of the twentieth century, the fight against prejudice continued. Martin Luther King, Jr.'s 1963 "I Have a Dream" speech and, three years later, César Chávez's moving words to Mexican farmworkers in California represent that struggle, a struggle that challenges America to this day.

Some words resound beyond a nation's borders. John F. Kennedy admitted in his speech at the Berlin Wall in 1963 that "freedom has many difficulties and democracy is not perfect." He went on to say that "freedom is indivisible, and when one man is enslaved, all are not free." And when Hillary Rodham Clinton spoke at the United Nations Conference on Women in Beijing, China, in 1995, her message was not only about women's rights but about the rights of all people around the world.

The same words that govern the personal freedoms of America's citizens also define the United States to the rest of the world. Indeed, in the eyes of the civil rights activists in South Africa and the students who rallied in Tiananmen Square, America is freedom. Our documents, our words inspire their actions. And, in an age when television and the Internet influence much of what we do, we must learn to govern them. The ideals of free speech and the civil rights promised to all Americans must be guaranteed in these evolving media as well. And where better to look for these guidelines than in the words of American history?

Although Paul Revere and his friends did not argue on behalf of human rights or petition to restructure the government of the colonies, they did find a way to voice their simple dream. So it is in the excerpts presented here that we find the voices that created the nation we are now—the same voices that will shape the nation we become.

THE MAYFLOWER COMPACT

(NOVEMBER 11, 1620)

In this illustration the Pilgrims gather around a table to sign the Mayflower Compact. The Compact was used to govern the settlement until Plymouth became part of the Massachusetts Bay Colony in 1691. The baby in the cradle, Peregrine White, was the first English baby born in New England. He was born on board the Mayflower *on November 20, 1620, as the ship was off Cape Cod Harbor.*

About one-third of the passengers on the Mayflower *were English Separatists—men and women who had separated themselves from the Church of England because they believed it was corrupt. Most Separatists were farmers and craftworkers.*

After 65 days on rough seas, with 102 people aboard, the sailing ship *Mayflower* approached Cape Cod, Massachusetts. Storms and errors had forced the ship far off course from Virginia, its original destination. During the long voyage the passengers had overcome many crises. Now, exhausted and weakened by poor diet and illness, they faced a new challenge.

The "Pilgrims," as 88 of the passengers were called, had received a charter allowing them to establish a colony in Virginia. Now they were about to build a colony far to the north, where they had no legal right to settle. They realized that for their settlement to survive they must immediately agree on an orderly way to govern it. So, on November 11, 1620, 41 of the adult males on board signed an agreement called the Mayflower Compact.

They pledged to form a government that would make just and equal laws that they agreed to obey. The Mayflower Compact was the first document of self-government for North America.

In the name of God Amen. We whose names are underwritten, the loyall subjects of our dread soveraigne Lord King James by the grace of God, of great Britaine, France, & Ireland king, defender of the faith, &c.

Haveing undertaken, for the glorie of God, and advancements of the Christian faith and honour of our king & countrie, a voyage to plant the first colonie in the Northerne parts of Virginia, doe by these presents solemnly & mutualy in the presence of God, and one of another, covenant & combine our selves togeather into a civill body politick; for our better ordering, & preservation & furtherance of the ends aforesaid; and by vertue hearof to enacte, constitute, and frame shuch just & equall lawes, ordinances, Acts, constitutions, & offices, from time to time, as shall be thought most meete & convenient for the generall good of the Colonie: unto which we promise all due submission and obedience.

In witnes whereof we have hereunder subscribed our names at Cap-Codd the • 11 • of November, in the year the raigne of our soveraigne Lord King James of England, France, & Ireland, the eighteenth and of Scotland the fiftie fourth, An°: Dom. 1620.

John Winthrop was the first governor of the Massachusetts Bay Colony, founded nine years after the Pilgrims landed in Plymouth, Massachusetts.

The colonists came ashore on December 26, 1620, at Plymouth. William Bradford, one of their leaders, later recalled that "the whole country, full of woods and thickets, represented a savage hue."

AUTHORS

There were 102 men and women aboard the *Mayflower*. The adult male signers did not include the servants and seamen. Women could not sign because they had no political rights.

RESPONSE

The new colony was too small and too far away for a great European power such as England to pay attention to it. During town meetings the local colonial government relied on the Mayflower Compact to pass laws, elect assistants to the governor, and add new voters.

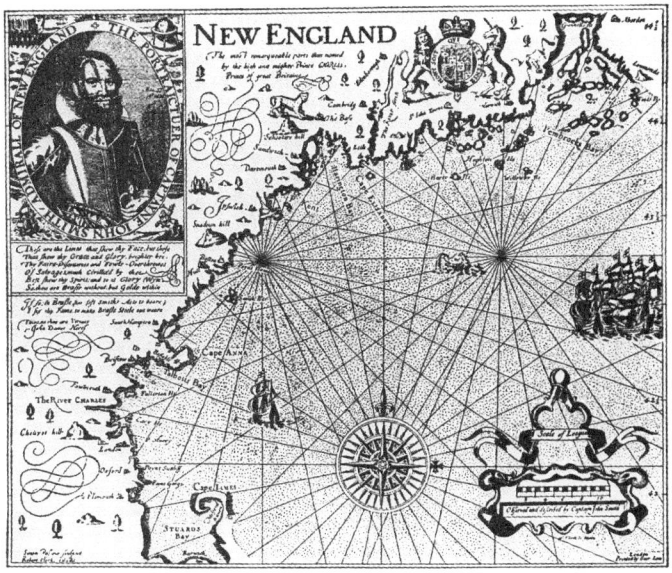

Explorer John Smith was one of the leaders of the English colony at Jamestown, Virginia. In 1614 he sailed along the northeast coast and in 1616 made this map of the region he named New England.

Poor Richard's Almanack

(1733–1758)

Benjamin Franklin

This engraving depicts Benjamin Franklin, at right, working as an apprentice in Boston in the printer's shop of his older brother James. During colonial times, apprentices training for a job did not receive a salary but did get food and lodging.

Benjamin Franklin published this annual almanac in Philadelphia. It contained a calendar, weather predictions, recipes, medical advice, farming tips, and an astrological guide. Franklin also included Poor Richard's proverbs—brief, clever sayings related to daily life. These sayings reflected the value of hard work and common sense. The following proverbs are from Franklin's almanac.

When he was twelve years old, Franklin began working for his brother James. Soon he was writing essays for James's newspapers. The young Franklin never signed his own name to these essays but used made-up names. This was a common practice in his day.

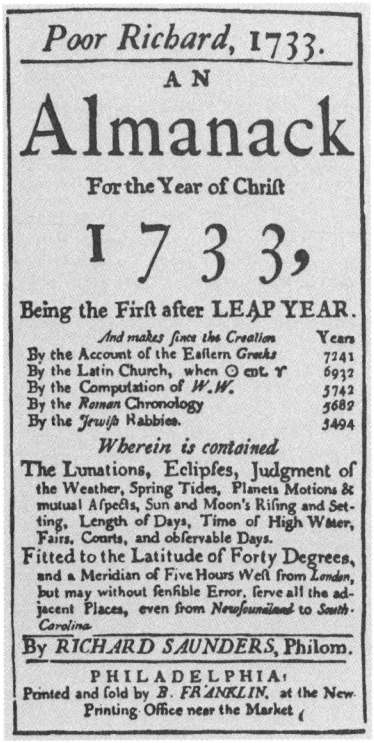

Poor Richard, 1733.

AN

Almanack

For the Year of Chrift

1733,

Being the Firft after LEAP YEAR.

And makes fince the Creation	Years
By the Account of the Eaftern *Greeks*	7241
By the Latin Church, when ♋ ent. ♈	6932
By the Computation of *W.W.*	5742
By the *Roman* Chronology	5682
By the *Jewifh* Rabbies.	5494

Wherein is contained

The Lunations, Eclipfes, Judgment of the Weather, Spring Tides, Planets Motions & mutual Afpects, Sun and Moon's Rifing and Setting, Length of Days, Time of High Water, Fairs, Courts, and obfervable Days.

Fitted to the Latitude of Forty Degrees, and a Meridian of Five Hours Weft from *London*, but may without fenfible Error, ferve all the adjacent Places, even from *Newfoundland* to *South-Carolina*.

By *RICHARD SAUNDERS*, Philom.

PHILADELPHIA:
Printed and fold by *B. FRANKLIN*, at the New-Printing-Office near the Market.

This is the cover of the first edition of Poor Richard's Almanack.

He that waits upon a Fortune, is never sure of a Dinner.

Keep thy shop, and thy shop will keep thee.

Three may keep a secret if two of them are dead.

Early to bed and early to rise, makes a man healthy wealthy and wise.

Diligence is the Mother of Good-Luck.

Do not do that which you would not have known.

Wealth is not his that has it, but his that enjoys it.

God helps them that help themselves.

Don't throw stones at your neighbours, if your own windows are glass.

The seventy-eight-year-old Benjamin Franklin, pictured with hat, visits workers at the printer's shop where he worked in Philadelphia after he moved from Boston at the age of seventeen.

AUTHOR

Benjamin Franklin (1706–1790) is considered one of the greatest Americans. Born in Boston, Franklin was a self-educated man. A printer, author, patriot, politician, diplomat, inventor, scientist, and philosopher, he was interested in many things. In 1723 Franklin moved to Philadelphia, where he began printing a newspaper, books, and *Poor Richard's Almanack.* Franklin was so successful that he was able to give up active control of his printing business in 1848, when he was forty-two years old. For the rest of his life he devoted himself to other interests.

RESPONSE

Almanacs were extremely popular colonial reading matter. Of all the colonial almanacs, Franklin's is the best known, even though Franklin did not make up all the proverbs and sayings in *Poor Richard's Almanack*. He borrowed many from popular sayings and the Bible, often rewriting them. More colonists read *Poor Richard's Almanack* than any other publication except the Bible.

Franklin did not use his own name in publishing the almanac. Rather, he wrote under the fictional name of Richard Saunders. Unlike the sophisticated Franklin, Saunders was supposed to be a simple man, the "Poor Richard" ordinary readers could relate to.

SPEECH TO THE SECOND VIRGINIA CONVENTION

(MARCH 23, 1775)

PATRICK HENRY

In 1765 the English Parliament passed the Stamp Act. The act gave the British the power to tax all printed colonial documents, including newspapers, almanacs, and legal documents. Many colonists were furious because they felt they should not be taxed without their consent. Henry spoke in the Virginia legislature against the act. His speech was interrupted by cries of "Treason! Treason!" from legislators loyal to the king. Henry immediately replied, "If this be treason, make the most of it."

Patrick Henry's fiery temperament and passionate speeches had a strong impact on his listeners.

Patrick Henry was a leader in the revolutionary cause. On March 23, 1775, he made a stirring speech at the Second Virginia Convention at St. John's Church in Richmond, Virginia. Henry urged his listeners to support arming Virginia's militia to fight against England. The speech's greatness lies in its powerful statement of the ideals of liberty that lie at the heart of American democracy.

Subsequent generations of American schoolchildren were often required to memorize the entire speech or parts of it, especially the electrifying closing words, "give me liberty, or give me death." The following selection is from Henry's famous speech.

Patrick Henry made his famous 1775 speech to the Second Virginia Convention while they met in a church, not in their official building. The English governor of the colony had shut down the legislature after Henry's speech against the Stamp Act 10 years earlier, but the legislators continued to meet on their own. In this engraving, the Assembly reacts to Henry's speech.

I have but one lamp by which my feet are guided; and that is the lamp of experience. I know of no way of judging of the future but by the past. And judging by the past, I wish to know what there has been in the conduct of the British ministry for the last ten years to justify those hopes with which gentlemen have been pleased to solace themselves and the House? Is it that insidious smile with which our petition has been lately received? Trust it not, sir; it will prove a snare to your feet. Suffer not yourselves to be betrayed with a kiss. Ask yourselves how this gracious reception of our petition comports with these warlike preparations which cover our waters and darken our land. Are fleets and armies necessary to a work of love and reconciliation? Have we shown ourselves so unwilling to be reconciled, that force must be called in to win back our love? Let us not deceive ourselves, sir. These are the implements of war and subjugation; the last arguments to which kings resort. I ask gentlemen, sir, what means this martial array, if its purpose be not to force us to submission? Can

One observer said about Patrick Henry, "He is by far the most powerful speaker I ever heard. Every word he says not only engages, but commands the attention. . . ."

gentlemen assign any other possible motives for it? Has Great Britain any enemy, in this quarter of the world, to call for all this accumulation of navies and armies? No, sir, she has none. They are meant for us; they can be meant for no other. They are sent over to bind and rivet upon us those chains which the British ministry have been so long forging. And what have we to oppose to them? Shall we try argument? Sir, we have been trying that for the last ten years. Have we anything new to offer on the subject? Nothing. We have held the subject up in every light of which it is capable; but it has been all in vain. Shall we resort to entreaty and humble supplication? What terms shall we find which have not been already exhausted? Let us not, I beseech you, sir, deceive ourselves longer. Sir, we have done everything that could be done to avert the storm which is now coming on. . . . There is no longer any room for hope. If we wish to be free—if we mean to preserve inviolate those inestimable privileges for which we have been so long contending—if we mean not basely to abandon the noble struggle in which we have been so long engaged, and which we have pledged ourselves never to abandon until the glorious object of our contest shall be obtained, we must fight! I repeat it, sir, we must fight! An appeal to arms and to the God of Hosts is all that is left us!

Colonial silversmith and artist Paul Revere etched this 1765 engraving in copper, which allowed it to be printed again and again. The engraving shows the hanging of a fake body, representing John Huske, an American-born member of Parliament who supported the Stamp Act. Patriots such as Revere were angry at anyone who backed the act. The sign on the tree names it the "Liberty Tree." The sign also gives the date of the first demonstration by the colonists against the Stamp Act in Boston: August 14, 1765.

They tell us, sir, that we are weak; . . .Sir, we are not weak, if we make a proper use of the means which the God of nature hath placed in our power. Three millions of people, armed in the holy cause of liberty, and in such a country as that which we possess, are invincible by any force which our enemy can send against us. Besides, sir, we shall not fight our battles alone. There is a just God who presides over the destinies of nations; and who will raise friends to fight our battles for us. The battle, sir, is not to the strong alone; it is to the vigilant, the active, the brave. Besides, sir, we have no election. If we were base enough to desire it, it is now too late to retire from the contest. There is no retreat but in submission and slavery! Our chains are forged! Their clanking may be heard on the plains of Boston! The war is inevitable—and let it come! I repeat it, sir, let it come!

It is in vain, sir, to extenuate the matter. Gentlemen may cry peace, peace—but there is no peace. The war is actually begun! The next gale that sweeps from the North will bring to our ears the clash of resounding arms! Our brethren are already in the field! Why stand we here idle? What is it that gentlemen wish? What would they have? Is life so dear, or peace so sweet, as to be purchased at the price of chains and slavery? Forbid it, Almighty God! I know not what course others may take; but as for me, give me liberty, or give me death!

Henry refused to attend the Constitutional Convention in Philadelphia in May 1787, saying he "smelt a rat." Later, after the new Constitution was published, he complained, "Who authorized them to speak the language of We the people?" Henry also criticized the document for not containing a bill of rights. People listened. In 1789 Virginia's James Madison presented to Congress the amendments that became the Bill of Rights.

AUTHOR

Patrick Henry (1739–1799) became a member of the Virginia legislature in 1763. Born to a wealthy Virginia family, he tried farming and storekeeping and then became a lawyer. In the legislature, he spoke out passionately against British tyranny and demanded colonial independence. Henry was also a delegate to the First Continental Congress in 1774 and the Second Continental Congress in 1775. During and after the Revolution, he served five times as Virginia's governor.

RESPONSE

Henry's fiery speech helped move many colonists closer to the idea of independence from England.

COMMON SENSE

(JANUARY 10, 1776)

THOMAS PAINE

COMMON SENSE;

ADDRESSED TO THE

INHABITANTS

OF

AMERICA,

On the following interesting

SUBJECTS.

I. Of the Origin and Design of Government in general, with concise Remarks on the English Constitution.

II. Of Monarchy and Hereditary Succession.

III. Thoughts on the present State of American Affairs.

IV. Of the present Ability of America, with some miscellaneous Reflections.

A NEW EDITION, with several Additions in the Body of the Work. To which is added an APPENDIX; together with an Address to the People called QUAKERS.

N. B. The New Addition here given increases the Work upwards of one Third.

Man knows no Master save creating HEAVEN,
Or those whom Choice and common Good ordain.

The two-line poem on the bottom of the title page of Thomas Paine's Common Sense *reads "Man knows no Master save creating Heaven,/ Or those whom choice and common good ordain." The poem suggests that the American colonies should be ruled by only God or rulers they freely choose and who want what is best for most people. Here Paine is clearly saying that the colonists should not accept English rule because the common good of the colonies is of no interest to Great Britain.*

When Thomas Paine's 50-page pamphlet *Common Sense* was published, he had only been in America for a little more than a year. Paine, who had emigrated from England, had quickly become sympathetic to the colonial cause. Many colonists wanted to revolt against being unfairly taxed. If Great Britain surrendered to their demands, they were willing to remain English colonists. But Paine took things one step further. He advocated total independence from Great Britain. He presented his arguments in *Common Sense*.

The pamphlet became one of the most influential pieces of revolutionary writing. It persuaded ordinary colonists to fight for their independence from England. During Paine's lifetime and afterward, the pamphlet's fame spread beyond the American colonies. It helped oppressed people everywhere understand they had the right to fight for their own freedom.

I have heard it asserted by some, that as America hath flourished under her former connection with Great Britain, the same connection is necessary towards her future happiness, and will always have the same effect. Nothing can be more fallacious than this kind of argument. We may as well assert that because a child has thriven upon milk, that it is never to have meat, or that the first twenty years of our lives is to become a precedent for the next twenty. But even this is admitting more than is true; for I answer roundly, that America would have flourished as much, and probably much more, had no European power taken any notice of her. The commerce by which she enriched herself are the necessaries of life, and will always have a market while eating is the custom of Europe.

But she has protected us, say some. That she hath engrossed us is true, and defended the continent at our expense as well as her own is admitted. . . .

Alas! we have been long led away by ancient prejudices, and made large sacrifices to superstition. We have boasted the protection of Great Britain without considering that her motive was *interest*, not *attachment*; and that she did not protect us from *our enemies* on *our account*, but from her enemies on her own account, from those who had no quarrel with us on any *other account*, but who will always be our enemies on the *same account*. Let Britain waive her pretensions to the continent, or the continent throw off the dependence, and we should be at peace with France and Spain were they at war with Britain. . . .

But Britain is the parent country, say some. Then the more shame upon her conduct. Even brutes do not devour their young, nor savages make war upon their families; wherefore, the assertion, if true, turns to her reproach; but it happens not to be true, or only partly so, and the phrase *parent* or *mother country* hath been jesuitically adopted by the king and his parasites, with a low, papistical design of gaining an unfair bias on the credulous weakness of our minds. Europe, and not England, is the parent country of America. This new world hath been the asylum for the persecuted lovers of civil and religious liberty from every part of Europe. Hither have they fled, not from the tender embraces of a mother, but from the cruelty

In this engraving, the British troops arrive in Concord, Massachusetts, on April 19, 1775. Later, the troops met colonial Minutemen on the North Bridge. The battle that followed began the Revolutionary War.

Paine stopped going to school at the age of thirteen, when he became an apprentice in his father's corset shop in England. In 1757, after an unsuccessful attempt to run away to sea, he opened his own shop.

This is one of the few portraits of Paine still in existence.

In 1774 Paine met Benjamin Franklin in London. That year Franklin sent him to the American colonies with letters introducing Paine to Franklin's friends in Philadelphia.

of the monster; and it is so far true of England, that the same tyranny which drove the first emigrants from home, pursues their descendants still. . . .

I challenge the warmest advocate for reconciliation to show a single advantage that this continent can reap, by being connected with Great Britain. I repeat the challenge, not a single advantage is derived. Our corn will fetch its price in any market in Europe, and our imported goods must be paid for, buy them where we will. . . .

Every quiet method for peace hath been ineffectual. Our prayers have been rejected with disdain; and have tended to convince us that nothing flatters vanity or confirms obstinacy in kings more than repeated petitioning—and nothing hath contributed more than that very measure to make the kings of Europe absolute [have total power]. . . .Wherefore, since nothing but blows will do, for God's sake let us come to a final separation, and not leave the next generation to be cutting throats under the violated unmeaning names of parent and child.

To say they will never attempt it [English violations of the colonists' rights and property] again is idle and visionary; we thought so as the repeal of the stamp act, yet a year or two undeceived us; as well may we suppose that nations which have been once defeated will never renew the quarrel.

As to government matters, it is not in the power of Britain to do this continent justice: the business of it will soon be too weighty and intricate to be managed with any tolerable degree of convenience, by a power so distant from us, and so very ignorant of us; for if they cannot conquer us, they cannot govern us. . . .

Small islands not capable of protecting themselves are the proper objects for kingdoms to take under their care; but there is something very absurd in supposing a continent to be perpetually governed by an island. In no instance hath nature made the satellite larger than its primary planet; and as England and America, with respect to each other, reverse the common order of nature, it is evident that they belong to different systems. England to Europe: America to itself. . . .

But where, say some, is the king of America? I'll tell you, friend, he reigns above, and doth not make havoc of mankind like the Royal Brute of Great Britain. Yet that we may not appear to be defective even in earthly honors, let a day be solemnly set apart for proclaiming the charter; let it be brought forth placed on the divine law, the Word of God; let a crown be placed thereon, by which the world may know, that so far as we approve of monarchy, that in America THE LAW IS KING. For as in absolute governments the king is law, so in free countries the law ought to be king, and there ought to be no other. But lest any ill use should afterwards arise, let the crown at the conclusion of the ceremony be demolished, and scattered among the people whose right it is.

A government of our own is our natural right; and when a man seriously reflects on the precariousness of human affairs, he will become convinced, that it is infinitely wiser and safer to form a constitution of our own in a cool deliberate manner, while we have it in our power, than to trust such an interesting event to time and chance. . . .

O ye that love mankind! Ye that dare oppose not only the tyranny but the tyrant, stand forth! Every spot of the old world is overrun with oppression. Freedom hath been hunted round the globe. Asia and Africa have long expelled her. Europe regards her like a stranger, and England hath given her warning to depart. O receive the fugitive, and prepare in time an asylum for mankind.

Although Paine was a recent immigrant, he felt at home in colonial America and even served in the revolutionary army. Said Paine, "Where liberty is, there is my country."

AUTHOR

Thomas Paine (1737–1809) worked as a corset maker and as a tax collector in England before immigrating to Philadelphia in 1774. There, he became a journalist. After *Common Sense*, he wrote a series of pamphlets defending the American Revolution (1775–1783). One of these pamphlets, *The Crisis*, began with the famous phrase, "These are the times that try men's souls."

RESPONSE

Only three months after its publication in January 1776, 120,000 copies of *Common Sense* had been sold. The American population then numbered 2.5 million. One of every 20 people had a copy. Almost every colonist read this best-seller or heard it discussed.

LETTER TO JOHN ADAMS

(MARCH 31, 1776)

ABIGAIL ADAMS

This engraving of Abigail captures not only her beauty, but her force of character as well. Abigail Adams believed that "If we mean to have heroes, statesmen and philosophers, we should have learned women."

In March 1776 John Adams was in Philadelphia attending the Continental Congress. He left his wife, Abigail, and children behind at their Massachusetts farm. In this letter, Abigail gently but firmly reminds her husband that women should also have rights in the new nation, including the right to vote. When she wrote that women should vote, Abigail Adams was 154 years ahead of her time. American women gained this right in 1920, with the ratification of the Nineteenth Amendment.

Abigail Adams had a gift for writing. But it was almost impossible for colonial women to publish anything. They could, however, express themselves by writing letters, just as Abigail Adams did.

This engraving depicts women voting in New Jersey at the end of the eighteenth century.

. . . I long to hear that you have declared an independency—and by the way in the new Code of Laws which I suppose it will be necessary for you to make I desire you would Remember the Ladies, and be more generous and favourable to them than your ancestors. Do not put such unlimited power into the hands of the Husbands. Remember all Men would be tyrants if they could. If particular care and attention is not paid to the Ladies we are determined to foment a Rebellion, and will not hold ourselves bound by any Laws in which we have no voice, or Representation.

That your Sex are Naturally Tyrannical is a Truth so thoroughly established as to admit of no dispute, but such of you as wish to be happy willingly give up the harsh title of Master for the more tender and endearing one of Friend. Why then, not put it out of the power of the vicious and the Lawless to use us with cruelty and indignity with impunity. Men of Sense in all Ages abhor those customs which treat us only as the vassals [servants] of your Sex. Regard us then as Beings placed by providence under your protection and in imitation of the Supreme Being make use of that power only for our happiness.

Abigail Adams spoke frequently to her husband John about women's rights. In another letter, she said that men continued to insist on maintaining complete power over their wives. She then warned her husband, "But you must remember, that arbitrary power is like most other things which are very hard, very liable to be broken."

AUTHOR

Abigail Adams (1744–1818) was the wife of John Adams, who became the second president of the United States. Born in Massachusetts, she educated herself to a degree far beyond that of most colonial women. In 1764, at the age of nineteen, she married John Adams. Revolutionary politics required that her husband travel widely, often without her. While he was away, she took care of the farm and the household, bought land, and dealt with tenants. Their eldest son, John Quincy Adams, became the sixth president in 1824.

RESPONSE

Several months after Abigail composed the letter, Adams wrote to a lawyer named James Sullivan and declared that it was impossible for everyone to have the right to vote. He also said that women were unfit for political life but fit for caring for home and children.

For more than 40 years, Abigail Adams wrote letters to her husband and family.

New Jersey was the only state where women were allowed to vote. Its 1776 constitution granted the vote to anyone who possessed a certain amount of money. This phrasing accidentally permitted white widows and unmarried women who owned property to vote. But in 1807 the state legislature took away this right from women property-owners.

Declaration of Independence

(JULY 4, 1776)

In this painting Benjamin Franklin signs the Declaration of Independence, while Thomas Jefferson looks on at the left.

On June 11, 1776, the Second Continental Congress appointed a committee to draft a declaration of independence from England. The committee included Thomas Jefferson, Benjamin Franklin, and John Adams. Jefferson was asked by the committee to write the document. His draft justified American independence from England by listing the wrongs the mother country had inflicted on the colonists. Jefferson also sketched a basic philosophy of democratic government.

On June 28, the committee submitted Jefferson's draft to the Congress. The delegates debated and amended the declaration before approving it on July 4. Those who signed the document knew that they were committing treason against England and might possibly be executed for their crime. Nevertheless, every delegate to the Continental Congress signed the declaration.

The Declaration of Independence is considered to be one of the greatest documents of all time. The central section of the declaration is a ringing assertion that every human being has an equal right to life, liberty, and the pursuit of happiness.

The unanimous Declaration of the thirteen united States of America

When in the Course of human events, it becomes necessary for one people to dissolve the political bands which have connected them with another, and to assume among the Powers of the earth, the separate and equal station to which the Laws of Nature and of Nature's God entitle them, a decent respect to the opinions of mankind requires that they should declare the causes which impel them to the separation.—We hold these truths to be self-evident, that all men are created equal, that they are endowed by their Creator with certain unalienable Rights, that among these are Life, Liberty and the pursuit of Happiness.—That to secure these rights, Governments are instituted among Men, deriving their just powers from the consent of the governed,—That whenever any Form of Government becomes destructive of these ends, it is the Right of the People to alter or to abolish it, and to institute new Government, laying its foundation on such principles and organizing its powers in such form, as to them shall seem most likely to effect their Safety and Happiness. Prudence, indeed, will dictate that Governments long established should not be changed for light and transient causes; and accordingly all experience hath shewn, that mankind are more disposed to suffer, while evils are sufferable, than to right themselves by abolishing the forms to which they are accustomed. But when a long train of abuses and usurpations, pursuing invariably the same Object evinces a design to reduce them under absolute Despotism, it is their right, it is their duty, to throw off such Government, and to provide new Guards for their future security.—Such has been the patient sufferance of these Colonies; and such is now the necessity which constrains them to alter their former Systems of Government. The history of the present King of Great Britain is a history of repeated injuries and usurpations, all having in direct object the establishment of an absolute Tyranny over these States. To prove this, let Facts be submitted to a candid world.—He has refused his Assent to Laws, the most wholesome and necessary for the public good.—He has forbidden his Governors to pass Laws of immediate and

The Continental Congress never called the document the Declaration of Independence.

Jefferson wrote the draft on a portable writing desk that he pulled onto his lap at his lodgings on the outkirts of Philadelphia.

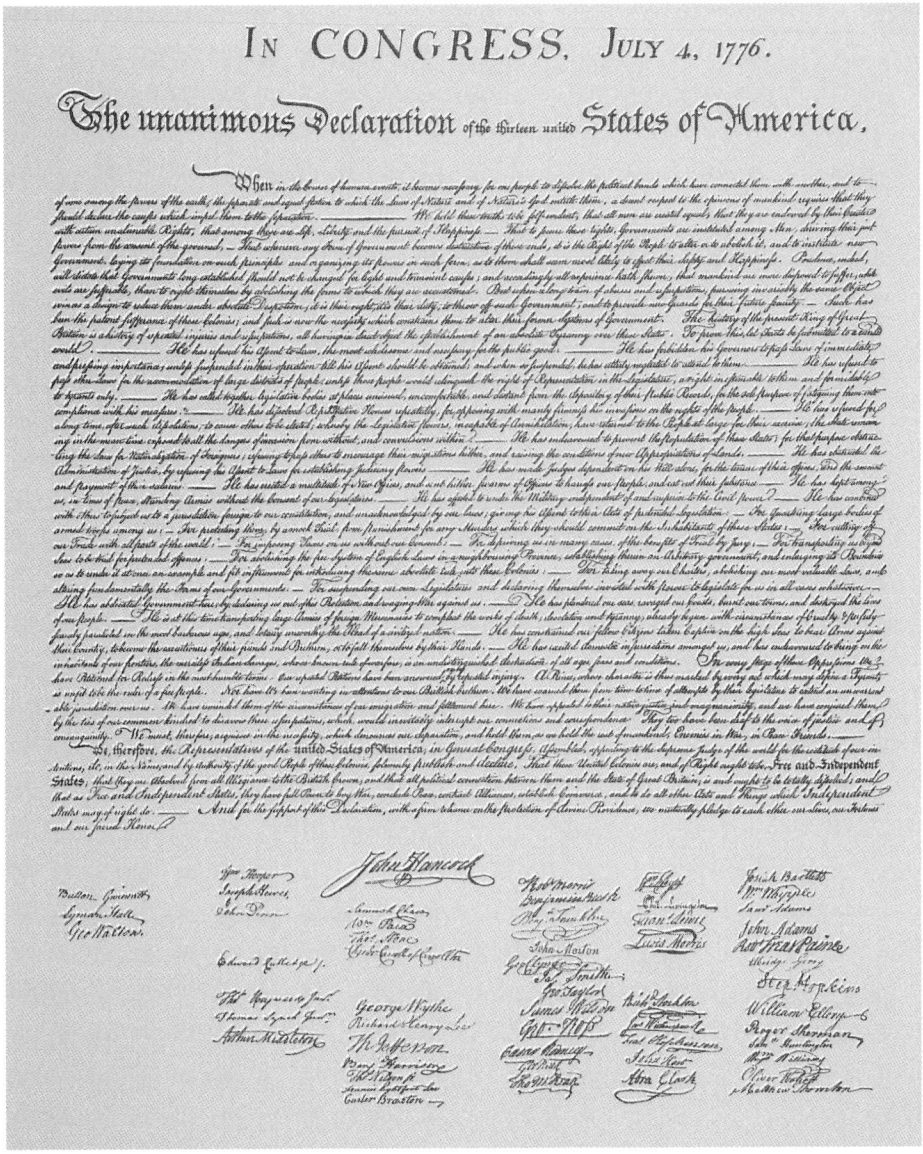

IN CONGRESS, JULY 4, 1776.

The unanimous Declaration of the thirteen united States of America,

The Declaration of Independence was first printed on July 4–5, 1776, by John Dunlap of Philadelphia, a printer to the Continental Congress.

pressing importance, unless suspended in their operation till his Assent should be obtained; and when so suspended, he has utterly neglected to attend to them.—He has refused to pass other Laws for the accommodation of large districts of people, unless those people would relinquish the right of Representation in the Legislature, a right inestimable to them and formidable to tyrants only.—He has called together legislative bodies at places unusual, uncomfortable, and distant from the depository of their public Records, for the sole purpose of fatiguing them into compliance with his measures.—He has dissolved Representative Houses repeatedly, for opposing with manly firmness his invasions on the rights of the people.—He has refused for a long time, after such dissolutions, to cause others to be elected; whereby the Legislative powers, incapable of Annihilation, have returned to the People at large for their exercise; the State remaining in the mean time exposed to all the dangers of invasion from without, and convulsions within.—He has endeavoured to prevent the population of these States; for that purpose obstructing the Laws for Naturalization of Foreigners; refusing to pass others to encourage their migrations hither, and raising the conditions of new Appropriations of Lands.—He has obstructed the Administration of Justice, by refusing his Assent to Laws for establishing Judiciary powers.—He has made Judges dependent on his Will alone, for the tenure of their offices, and the amount and payment of their salaries.—He has erected a multitude of New Offices, and sent hither swarms of Officers to harass our people, and eat out their substance.—He has kept among us, in times of peace, Standing Armies without the Consent of our legislatures.—He has affected to render the Military independent of and superior to the Civil power.—He has combined with others to subject us to a jurisdiction foreign to our constitution, and unacknowledged by our laws; giving his Assent to their Acts of pretended Legislation:—For quartering large bodies of armed troops among us:—For protecting them, by a mock Trial, from punishment for any Murders which they should commit on the Inhabitants of these States:—For cutting off our Trade with all parts of the world:—For imposing Taxes on us without our Consent:—For depriving us in many cases, of the benefits of Trial by Jury:—For transporting us beyond Seas to be tried for pretended offences:—For abolishing the free System of English Laws in a neighboring Province, establishing therein an Arbitrary government, and enlarging its Boundaries so as to render it at once an example and fit instrument for introducing the same absolute rule into these Colonies:—For taking away our Charters, abolishing our most valuable Laws, and altering fundamentally the Forms of our Governments:—For suspending our own Legislatures, and declaring themselves invested

Jefferson's first draft condemned England's King George III for "captivating and carrying" a "distant people" into slavery. Southern delegates agreed to support the declaration only if the slavery passage was removed.

with power to legislate for us in all cases whatsoever.—He has abdicated Government here, by declaring us out of his Protection and waging War against us.—He has plundered our seas, ravaged our Coasts, burnt our towns, and destroyed the Lives of our people.—He is at this time transporting large Armies of foreign Mercenaries to complete the works of death, desolation and tyranny, already begun with circumstances of Cruelty & perfidy scarcely paralleled in the most barbarous ages, and totally unworthy the Head of a civilized nation.—He has constrained our fellow Citizens taken Captive on the high Seas to bear Arms against their Country, to become the executioners of their friends and Brethren, or to fall themselves by their Hands.—He has excited domestic insurrections amongst us, and has endeavoured to bring on the inhabitants of our frontiers, the merciless Indian Savages, whose known rule of warfare, is an undistinguished destruction of all ages, sexes, and conditions. In every stage of these Oppressions We have Petitioned for Redress in the most humble terms: Our repeated Petitions have been answered only by repeated injury. A Prince, whose character is thus marked by every act which may define a Tyrant, is unfit to be the ruler of a free people. Nor have We been wanting in attentions to our British brethren. We have warned them from time to time of attempts by their legislature to extend an unwarrantable jurisdiction over us. We have reminded them of the circumstances of our emigration and settlement here. We have appealed to their native justice and magnanimity, and we have conjured them by the ties of our common kindred to disavow these usurpations, which, would inevitably interrupt our connections and correspondence. They too have been deaf to the voice of justice and of consanguinity. We must, therefore, acquiesce in the necessity, which denounces our Separation, and hold them, as we hold the result of mankind, Enemies in War, in Peace Friends.—

We therefore, the Representatives of the *United States of America*, in General Congress, Assembled, appealing to the Supreme Judge of the world for the rectitude of our intentions, do, in the Name, and by Authority of the good People of these Colonies, solemnly publish and declare, That these United Colonies are, and of Right ought to be *Free and Independent*

Thomas Jefferson at first doubted that he was skillful enough to draft the declaration, but other delegates he respected convinced him that he was the right person for the job.

States; that they are Absolved from all Allegiance to the British Crown, and that all political connection between them and the State of Great Britain, is and ought to be totally dissolved; and that as Free and Independent States, they have full Power to levy War, conclude Peace, contract Alliances, establish Commerce, and to do all other Acts and Things which Independent States may of right do.—And for the support of this Declaration, with a firm reliance on the protection of divine Providence, we mutually pledge to each other our Lives, our Fortunes and our sacred Honor.

The Declaration of Independence was approved by Congress on July 4, 1776, but the men who signed it on that day, Charles Thomson and John Hancock, signed only a draft. The official parchment copy was not signed by the delegates until August 2.

AUTHOR

Thomas Jefferson (1743–1826) was a young Virginia planter and lawyer when he wrote the Declaration of Independence. But he already had the reputation of being a skilled writer. Jefferson wanted John Adams to write the draft; but Adams said, "You can write ten times better than I." The democratic ideals Jefferson included were popular among liberal thinkers of his time. But they had never been used by a people to justify their right to rise up against their ruler and establish their own independent government. In 1801 Jefferson became the third president of the United States.

RESPONSE

France recognized the new nation in 1778. But the rest of Europe did not, fearing British anger. And of course England itself refused to recognize American independence until it lost the Revolutionary War in 1781. In the 1783 Treaty of Paris, which formally ended the war, Great Britain acknowledged the United States to be "free, sovereign, and independent."

In the eighteenth century, Independence Hall (or the State House) in Philadelphia was the site of several important assemblies opposing British policies. In addition to the Constitutional Convention in 1787, the Second Continental Congress met at Independence Hall in 1775 and the Declaration of Independence was signed there in 1776.

THE CONSTITUTION

(SEPTEMBER 17, 1787)

THE BILL OF RIGHTS

(SEPTEMBER 25, 1789)

On May 25, 1787, 55 delegates from 12 states (every state except Rhode Island) met at the State House in Philadelphia to revise the Articles of Confederation. The need for revision was urgent because the government had no power to regulate commerce or tax. Soon, however, the delegates decided to write a new constitution. This version focused on establishing a strong national government and a "checks and balances" system among the three branches of government (legislative, executive, and judiciary). A few individuals objected, arguing that individual rights were being neglected.

In order to gain support for the Constitution, James Madison promised to add amendments after ratification. Keeping his promise, he presented a drafted set of amendments to the House of Representatives on June 8, 1789, claiming they would protect "the great rights of mankind." After both

houses of Congress passed 12 of the amendments, the states ratified 10 of them and the Bill of Rights was added to the Constitution in 1791.

The Constitution is the oldest written national constitution in the world. Once ratified, the American people soon recognized the document's greatness, universally accepting it as the "supreme law of the land."

The Bill of Rights is universally admired as one of the world's greatest documents protecting individual liberties. It defined and secured the individual rights of Americans without weakening the Constitution. Although the Constitution has been amended twenty-seven times, the Bill of Rights has remained untouched.

The entire Constitution is on display at the National Archives in Washington, D.C., only once a year—September 17, the anniversary of the date it was signed. The other days of the year pages one and four are displayed in a bulletproof case. At night the pages are lowered into a vault with doors so thick, they can withstand a nuclear explosion.

We the People of the United States, in Order to form a more perfect Union, establish Justice, insure domestic Tranquility, provide for the common defense, promote the general Welfare, and secure the Blessings of Liberty to ourselves and our Posterity, do ordain and establish this Constitution for the United States of America.

Article I.

Section 1. All legislative Powers herein granted shall be vested in a Congress of the United States, which shall consist of a Senate and House of Representatives.

Section 2. The House of Representatives shall be composed of Members chosen every second Year by the People of the several States, and the Electors in each State shall have the Qualifications requisite for Electors of the most numerous Branch of the State Legislature.

No Person shall be a Representative who shall not have attained to the Age of twenty five Years, and been seven Years a Citizen of the United States, and who shall not, when elected, be an Inhabitant of that State in which he shall be chosen.

Representatives and direct Taxes shall be apportioned among the several States which may be included within this Union, according to their respective Numbers, which shall be determined by adding to the whole Number of free Persons, including those bound to Service for a Term of Years, and excluding Indians not taxed, three fifths of all other Persons. The actual Enumeration shall be made within three Years after the first Meeting of the Congress of the United States, and within every subsequent Term of ten Years, in such Manner as they shall by Law direct. The Number of Representatives shall not exceed one for every thirty Thousand, but each State shall have at least one Representative; and until such Enumeration shall be made, the State of New Hampshire shall be entitled to chuse three, Massachusetts eight, Rhode Island and Providence Plantations one, Connecticut five, New York six, New Jersey four, Pennsylvania eight, Delaware one, Maryland six, Virginia ten, North Carolina five, South Carolina five, and Georgia three.

When vacancies happen in the Representation from any State, the Executive Authority thereof shall issue Writs of Election to fill such Vacancies.

The House of Representatives shall chuse their Speaker and other Officers; and shall have the sole Power of Impeachment.

Section 3. The Senate of the United States shall be composed of two Senators from each State, chosen by the Legislature thereof, for six Years; and each Senator shall have one Vote.

Immediately after they shall be assembled in Consequence of the first Election, they shall be divided as equally as may be into three Classes. The Seats of the Senators of the first Class shall be vacated at the Expiration of the second Year, of the second Class at the Expiration of the fourth Year, and of the third Class at the Expiration of the sixth Year, so that one third may be chosen every second Year; and if Vacancies happen by Resignation, or otherwise, during the Recess of the Legislature of any State, the Executive thereof may make temporary Appointments until the next Meeting of the Legislature, which shall then fill such Vacancies.

No Person shall be a Senator who shall not have attained to the Age of thirty Years, and been nine Years a Citizen of the United States, and who shall not, when elected, be an Inhabitant of that State for which he shall be chosen.

The Vice President of the United States shall be President of the Senate, but shall have no Vote, unless they be equally divided.

The Senate shall chuse their other Officers, and also a President pro tempore, in the Absence of the Vice President, or when he shall exercise the Office of President of the United States.

The Senate shall have the sole Power to try all Impeachments. When sitting for that Purpose, they shall be on Oath or Affirmation. When the President of the United States is tried, the Chief Justice shall preside: And no Person shall be convicted without the Concurrence of two thirds of the Members present.

Judgment in Cases of Impeachment shall not extend further than to removal from Office, and disqualification to hold and enjoy any Office of Honor, Trust or Profit under the United States: but the Party convicted shall nevertheless be liable and subject to Indictment, Trial, Judgment and Punishment, according to Law.

Section 4. The Times, Places and Manner of holding Elections for Senators and Representatives, shall be prescribed in each State by the Legislature thereof; but the Congress may at any time by Law make or alter such Regulations, except as to the Places of chusing Senators.

The Congress shall assemble at least once in every Year, and such Meeting shall be on the first Monday in December, unless they shall by Law appoint a different Day.

Section 5. Each House shall be the Judge of the Elections, Returns and Qualifications of its own Members, and a Majority of each shall constitute a Quorum to do Business; but a smaller Number may adjourn from day to day, and may be authorized to compel the Attendance of absent Members, in such Manner, and under such Penalties as each House may provide.

Each House may determine the Rules of its Proceedings, punish its Members for disorderly Behaviour, and with the Concurrence of two thirds, expel a Member.

Each House shall keep a Journal of its Proceedings, and from time to time publish the same, excepting such Parts as may in their Judgment require Secrecy; and the Yeas and Nays of the Members of either House on any question shall, at the Desire of one fifth of those Present, be entered on the Journal.

Neither House, during the Session of Congress, shall without the Consent of the other, adjourn for more than three days, nor to any other Place than that in which the two Houses shall be sitting.

Section 6. The Senators and Representatives shall receive a Compensation for their Services, to be ascertained by Law, and paid out of the Treasury of the United States. They shall in all Cases, except Treason, Felony and Breach of the Peace, be privileged from Arrest during their Attendance at the Session of their respective Houses, and in going to and returning from the same; and for any Speech or Debate in either House, they shall not be questioned in any other Place.

No Senator or Representative shall, during the Time for which he was elected, be appointed to any civil Office under the Authority of the United States, which shall have been created, or the Emoluments whereof shall have been encreased during such time; and no Person holding any Office under the United States, shall be a Member of either House during his Continuance in Office.

Section 7. All Bills for raising Revenue shall originate in the House of Representatives; but the Senate may propose or concur with Amendments as on other Bills.

Every Bill which shall have passed the House of Representatives and the Senate, shall, before it become a Law, be presented to the President of the United States; if he approve he shall sign it, but if not he shall return it, with his Objections to that House in which it shall have originated, who shall enter the Objections at large on their Journal, and proceed to reconsider it. If after such Reconsideration two thirds of that House shall agree to pass the Bill, it shall be sent, together with the Objections, to the other House, by which it shall likewise be reconsidered, and if approved by two thirds of that House, it shall become a Law. But in all such Cases the Votes of both Houses shall be determined by Yeas and Nays, and the Names of the Persons voting for and against the Bill shall be entered on the Journal of each House respectively. If any Bill shall not be returned by the President within ten Days (Sundays excepted) after it shall have been presented to him, the same shall be a Law, in like Manner as if he had signed it, unless the Congress by their Adjournment prevent its Return, in which Case it shall not be a Law.

Every Order, Resolution, or Vote to which the Concurrence of the Senate and House of Representatives may be necessary (except on a question of Adjournment) shall be presented to the President of the United States; and before the same shall take Effect, shall be approved by him, or being disapproved by him, shall be repassed by two thirds of the Senate and House of Representatives, according to the Rules and Limitations prescribed in the Case of a Bill.

This photo shows the first page of the Constitution.

WE THE PEOPLE of the United States, in order to form a more perfect Union, establish Justice, insure domestic Tranquility, provide for the common defence, promote the general Welfare, and secure the Blessings of Liberty to ourselves and our Posterity, do ordain and establish this Constitution for the United States of America.

ARTICLE I.

Section 1. All legislative Powers herein granted shall be vested in a Congress of the United States, which shall consist of a Senate and House of Representatives.

Section 2. The House of Representatives shall be composed of Members chosen every second Year by the People of the several States, and the Electors in each State shall have the Qualifications requisite for Electors of the most numerous Branch of the State Legislature.

No Person shall be a Representative who shall not have attained to the Age of twenty-five Years, and been seven Years a Citizen of the United States, and who shall not, when elected, be an Inhabitant of that State in which he shall be chosen.

Representatives and direct Taxes shall be apportioned among the several States which may be included within this Union, according to their respective Numbers, which shall be determined by adding to the whole Number of free Persons, including those bound to Service for a Term of Years, and excluding Indians not taxed, three-fifths of all other Persons [Modified by Amendment XIV]. The actual Enumeration shall be made within three Years after the first Meeting of the Congress of the United States, and within every subsequent Term of ten Years, in such Manner as they shall by Law direct. The Number of Representatives shall not exceed one for every thirty Thousand, but each State shall have at Least one Representative; and until such enumeration shall be made, the State of New Hampshire shall be entitled to choose three, Massachusetts eight, Rhode-Island and Providence Plantations one, Connecticut five, New-York six, New Jersey four, Pennsylvania eight, Delaware one, Maryland six, Virginia ten, North Carolina five, South Carolina five, and Georgia three.

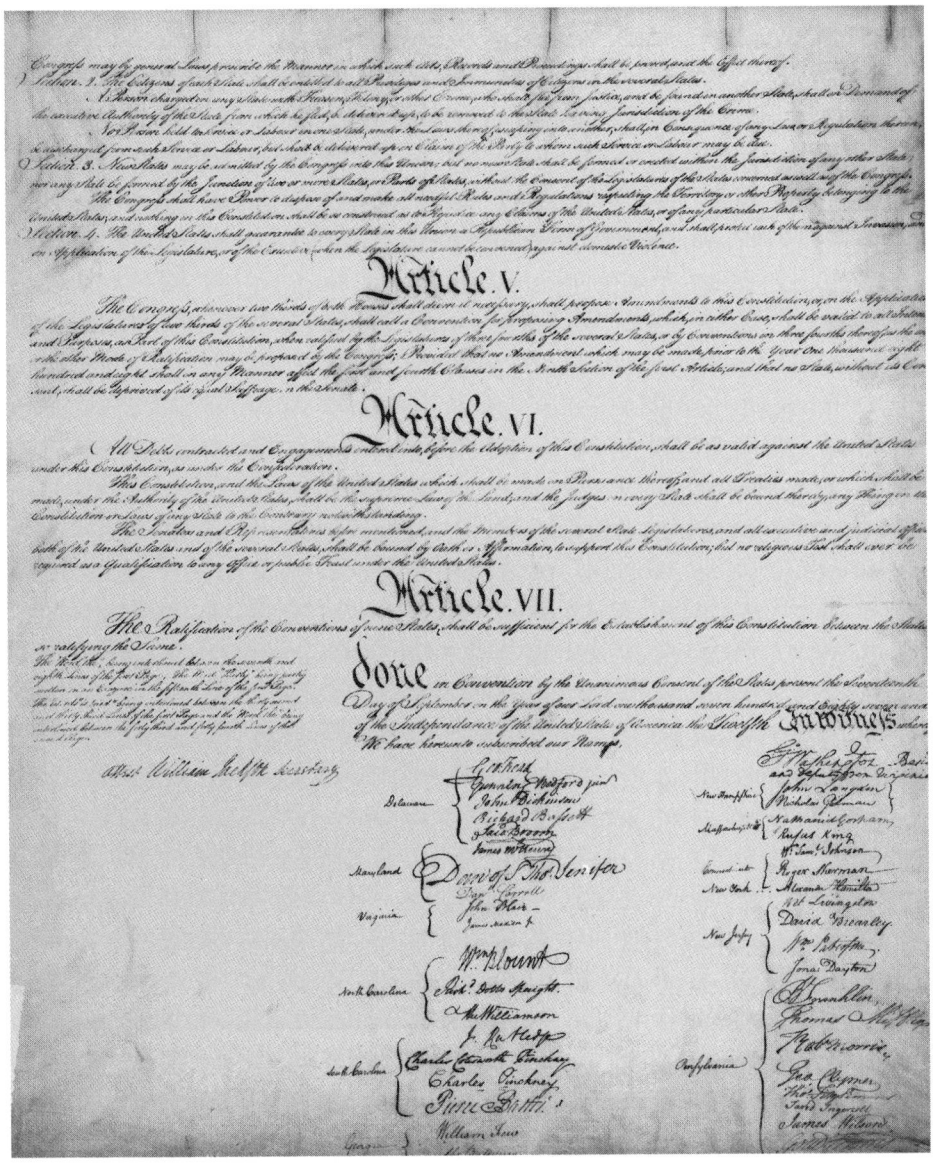

This photo shows the last page of the Constitution.

A total of 39 men signed the Constitution. George Washington was not one of them.

When vacancies happen in the Representation from any State, the Executive Authority thereof shall issue Writs of Election to fill such Vacancies. The House of Representatives shall choose their Speaker and other Officers; and shall have the sole Power of Impeachment.

Section 3. The Senate of the United States shall be composed of two Senators from each State, chosen by the Legislature thereof [Modified by Amendment XVII], for six Years; and each Senator shall have one Vote.

Immediately after they shall be assembled in Consequence of the first Election, they shall be divided as equally as may be

Before the Philadelphia meeting, James Madison bought and then carefully read more than two hundred books on history and government to prepare for writing the Constitution.

into three Classes. The Seats of the Senators of the first Class shall be vacated at the Expiration of the second Year, of the second Class at the Expiration of the fourth Year, and of the third Class at the Expiration of the sixth Year, so that one-third may be chosen every second Year; and if Vacancies happen by Resignation, or otherwise, during the Recess of the Legislature of any State, the Executive thereof may make temporary Appointments until the next Meeting of the Legislature, which shall then fill such Vacancies [Modified by Amendment XVII].

No Person shall be a Senator who shall not have attained to the Age of thirty Years, and been nine Years a Citizen of the United States, and who shall not, when elected, be an Inhabitant of that State for which he shall be chosen.

The Vice President of the United States shall be President of the Senate, but shall have no Vote, unless they be equally divided.

The Senate shall choose their other Officers, and also a President pro tempore, in the Absence of the Vice President, or when he shall exercise the Office of President of the United States.

The Senate shall have the sole Power to try all Impeachments. When sitting for that Purpose, they shall be on Oath or Affirmation. When the President of the United States is tried, the Chief Justice shall preside: And no Person shall be convicted without the Concurrence of two thirds of the Members present.

Judgment in Cases of Impeachment shall not extend further than to removal from Office, and disqualification to hold and enjoy any Office of honor, Trust or Profit under the United States: but the Party convicted shall nevertheless be liable and subject to Indictment, Trial, Judgment and Punishment, according to Law.

Section 4. The Times, Places and Manner of holding Elections for Senators and Representatives, shall be prescribed in each State by the Legislature thereof; but the Congress may at any time by Law make or alter such Regulations, except as to the Places of choosing Senators.

The Congress shall assemble at least once in every Year, and such Meeting shall be on the first Monday in December [Modified by Amendment XX], unless they shall by Law appoint a different Day.

Section 5. Each House shall be the Judge of the Elections, Returns and Qualifications of its own Members, and a Majority of each shall constitute a Quorum to do Business; but a smaller Number may adjourn from day to day, and may be authorized to compel the Attendance of absent Members, in such Manner, and under such Penalties as each House may provide.

Each House may determine the Rules of its Proceedings, punish its Members for disorderly Behavior, and, with the Concurrence of two-thirds, expel a Member.

Each House shall keep a Journal of its Proceedings, and from time to time publish the same, excepting such Parts as may in their Judgment require Secrecy; and the Yeas and the Nays of the Members of either House on any question shall, at the Desire of one-fifth of those Present, be entered on the Journal.

Neither House, during the Session of Congress, shall, without the Consent of the other, adjourn for more than three days, nor to any other Place than that in which the two Houses shall be sitting.

Section 6. The Senators and Representatives shall receive a Compensation for their Services, to be ascertained by Law, and paid out of the Treasury of the United States. They shall in all Cases, except Treason, Felony and Breach of the Peace, be privileged from Arrest during their Attendance at the Session of their respective Houses, and in going to and returning from the same; and for any Speech or Debate in either House, they shall not be questioned in any other Place.

No Senator or Representative shall, during the Time for which he was elected, be appointed to any civil Office under the Authority of the United States, which shall have been created, or the Emoluments [compensation] whereof shall have been increased during such time; and no Person holding any Office under the United States, shall be a Member of either House during his Continuance in Office.

Section 7. All Bills for raising Revenue shall originate in the House of Representatives; but the Senate may propose or concur with Amendments as on other Bills.

Every Bill which shall have passed the House of Representatives and the Senate, shall, before it becomes a Law, be presented to the President of the United States; if he approve he shall sign it, but if not he shall return it, with his Objections

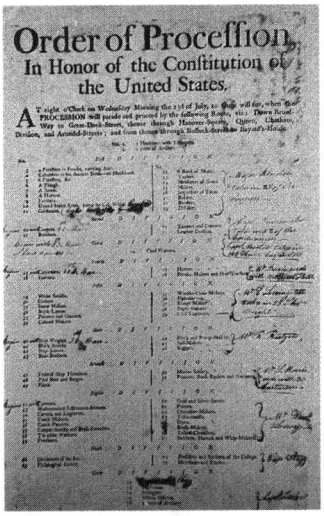
Order of Procession,
In Honor of the Constitution of the United States.

When the Constitution was finally ratified, there was a great celebration in New York City. This program, titled "Order of Procession in Honor of the Constitution of the United States," lists the order in which people would march in the parade, as well as the route to be taken through the city.

At just 4,440 words, the U.S. Constitution is the shortest document of its kind. It is also the oldest.

to that House in which it shall have originated, who shall enter the Objections at large on their Journal, and proceed to reconsider it. If after such Reconsideration two thirds of that House shall agree to pass the Bill, it shall be sent, together with the Objections, to the other House, by which it shall likewise be reconsidered, and if approved by two thirds of that House, it shall become a Law. But in all such Cases the Votes of both Houses shall be determined by yeas and Nays, and the Names of the Persons voting for and against the Bill shall be entered on the Journal of each House respectively. If any Bill shall not be returned by the President within ten Days (Sundays excepted) after it shall have been presented to him, the Same shall be a Law, in like Manner as if he had signed it, unless the Congress by their Adjournment prevent its Return, in which Case it shall not be a Law.

Every Order, Resolution, or Vote to which the Concurrence of the Senate and House of Representatives may be necessary (except on a question of Adjournment) shall be presented to the President of the United States; and before the Same shall take Effect, shall be approved by him, or being disapproved by him, shall be repassed by two thirds of the Senate and House of Representatives, according to the Rules and Limitations prescribed in the Case of a Bill.

Section 8. The Congress shall have Power To lay and collect Taxes, Duties, Imposts and Excises, to pay the Debts and provide for the common Defence and general Welfare of the United States; but all Duties, Imposts and Excises shall be uniform throughout the United States;

To borrow Money on the credit of the United States;

To regulate Commerce with foreign Nations, and among the several States, and with the Indian Tribes;

To establish an uniform Rule of Naturalization, and uniform Laws on the subject of Bankruptcies through out the United States;

To coin Money, regulate the Value thereof, and of foreign Coin, and fix the Standard of Weights and Measures;

To provide for the Punishment of counterfeiting the Securities and current Coin of the United States;

To establish Post Offices and post Roads;

To promote the Progress of Science and useful Arts, by securing for limited Times to Authors and Inventors the exclusive Right to their respective Writings and Discoveries;

To constitute Tribunals inferior to the supreme Court;

To define and punish Piracies and Felonies committed on the high Seas, and Offenses against the Law of Nations;

To declare War, grant Letters of Marque and Reprisal, and make Rules concerning Captures on Land and Water;

To raise and support Armies, but no Appropriation of Money to that Use shall be for a longer Term than two Years;

To provide and maintain a Navy;

To make Rules for the Government and Regulation of the land and naval Forces;

To provide for calling forth the Militia to execute the Laws of the Union, suppress Insurrections and repel Invasions;

To provide for organizing, arming, and disciplining the Militia, and for governing such Part of them as may be employed in the Service of the United States, reserving to the States respectively, the Appointment of the Officers, and the Authority of training the Militia according to the discipline prescribed by Congress;

To exercise exclusive Legislation in all Cases whatsoever, over such District (not exceeding ten Miles square) as may, by Cession of particular States, and the Acceptance of Congress, become the Seat of the Government of the United States, and to exercise like Authority over all Places purchased by the Consent of the Legislature of the State in which the Same shall be, for the Erection of Forts, Magazines, Arsenals, dock-Yards, and other needful Buildings;—And

To make all Laws which shall be necessary and proper for carrying into Execution the foregoing Powers, and all other Powers vested by this Constitution in the Government of the United States, or in any Department or Officer thereof.

Section 9. The Migration or Importation of such Persons as any of the States now existing shall think proper to admit, shall not be prohibited by the Congress prior to the Year one thousand eight hundred and eight, but a Tax or duty may be imposed on such Importation, not exceeding ten dollars for each Person.

The Privilege of the Writ of Habeas Corpus shall not be

Because they were serving as ambassadors in Europe, Thomas Jefferson and John Adams did not attend the Philadelphia meeting. But Jefferson praised the delegates as "an assembly of demigods."

suspended, unless when in Cases of Rebellion or Invasion the public Safety may require it.

No Bill of Attainder or ex post facto Law shall be passed.

No Capitation, or other direct, Tax shall be laid, unless in Proportion to the Census or Enumeration herein before directed to be taken.

No Tax or Duty shall be laid on Articles exported from any State.

No Preference shall be given by any Regulation of Commerce or Revenue to the Ports of one State over those of another: nor shall Vessels bound to, or from, one State, be obliged to enter, clear, or pay Duties in another.

No Money shall be drawn from the Treasury, but in Consequence of Appropriations made by Law; and a regular Statement and Account of the Receipts and Expenditures of all public Money shall be published from time to time.

No Title of Nobility shall be granted by the United States: And no Person holding any Office of Profit or Trust under them, shall, without the Consent of the Congress, accept of any present, Emolument, Office, or Title, of any kind whatever, from any King, Prince, or foreign State.

Section 10. No State shall enter into any Treaty, Alliance, or Confederation; grant Letters of Marque and Reprisal; coin Money; emit Bills of Credit; make any Thing but gold and silver Coin a Tender in Payment of Debts; pass any Bill of Attainder, ex post facto Law, or Law impairing the Obligation of Contracts, or grant any Title of Nobility.

No State shall, without the Consent of the Congress, lay any Imposts or Duties on Imports or Exports, except what may be absolutely necessary for executing its inspection Laws: and the net Produce of all Duties and Imposts, laid by any State on Imports or Exports, shall be for the Use of the Treasury of the United States; and all such Laws shall be subject to the Revision and Control of the Congress.

No State shall, without the Consent of Congress, lay any Duty of Tonnage, keep Troops, or Ships of War in time of Peace, enter into any Agreement or Compact with another State, or with a foreign Power, or engage in War, unless actually invaded, or in such imminent Danger as will not admit of delay.

At 5 feet 4 inches and less than 100 pounds, "the Father of the Constitution," James Madison, was too small to serve in the Revolutionary War, so he decided to pursue a career in politics instead.

Creating the Constitution was not easy. As represented in this painting, the delegates debated throughout the long, hot summer of 1787. Even George Washington (standing right) said that he saw no end in sight. Finally, in mid-September, the weary delegates signed the final document.

ARTICLE II.

Section 1. The executive Power shall be vested in a President of the United States of America. He shall hold his Office during the Term of four Years, and, together with the Vice President, chosen for the same Term, be elected, as follows:

Each State, shall appoint, in such Manner as the Legislature, thereof may direct, a Number of Electors, equal to the whole Number of Senators and Representatives to which the State may be entitled in the Congress; but no Senator or Representative, or Person holding an Office of Trust or Profit under the United States, shall be appointed an Elector.

The Electors shall meet in their respective States, and vote by Ballot for two Persons, of whom one at least shall not be an Inhabitant of the same State with themselves. And they shall make a List of all the Persons voted for, and of the Number of Votes for each; which List they shall sign and certify, and transmit sealed to the Seat of the Government of the United States, directed to the President of the Senate. The President of the Senate shall, in the Presence of the Senate and House of Representatives, open all the Certificates, and the Votes shall then be counted. The Person having the greatest Number of Votes shall be the President, if such Number be a Majority of the whole Number of Electors appointed; and if there be more than one who have such Majority, and have an equal Number of Votes, then the House of Representatives shall immediately choose by Ballot one of them for President; and if no Person have a Majority, then from the five highest on the List the said House shall in like Manner choose the President. But in choosing the President, the Votes shall be taken by States, the Representation from each State having one Vote; a quorum for this Purpose shall consist of a Member or Members from two-thirds of the States, and a Majority of all the States shall be necessary to a Choice. In every Case, after the Choice of the President, the Person having the greatest Number of Votes of the Electors shall be the Vice President. But if there should remain two or more who have equal Votes, the Senate shall choose from them by Ballot the Vice President [Modified by Amendment XII].

The Congress may determine the Time of choosing the Electors, and the Day on which they shall give their Votes; which Day shall be the same throughout the United States.

No Person except a natural born Citizen, or a Citizen of the United States, at the time of the Adoption of this Constitution, shall be eligible to the Office of President; neither shall any Person be eligible to that Office who shall not have attained to the Age of thirty-five Years, and been fourteen Years a Resident within the United States.

In Case of the Removal of the President from Office, or of his Death, Resignation, or Inability to discharge the Powers and Duties of the said Office, the Same shall devolve on the Vice President, and the Congress may by Law provide for the Case of Removal, Death, Resignation or Inability, both of the President and Vice President, declaring what Officer shall then act as President, and such Officer shall act accordingly, until the Disability be removed, or a President shall be elected [Modified by Amendment XXV].

The President shall, at stated Times, receive for his Services, a Compensation, which shall neither be increased nor diminished during the Period for which he shall have been elected, and he shall not receive within that Period any other Emolument from the United States, or any of them.

Before he enter on the Execution of his Office, he shall take the following Oath or Affirmation:—"I do solemnly swear (or affirm) that I will faithfully execute the Office of President of the United States, and will to the best of my Ability, preserve, protect and defend the Constitution of the United States."

Section 2. The President shall be Commander in Chief of the Army and Navy of the United States, and of the Militia of the several States, when called into the actual Service of the United States; he may require the Opinion, in writing, of the principal Officer in each of the executive Departments, upon any Subject relating to the Duties of their respective Offices, and he shall have Power to grant Reprieves and Pardons for Offenses against the United States, except in Cases of Impeachment.

He shall have Power, by and with the Advice and Consent of the Senate, to make Treaties, provided two-thirds of the Senators present concur; and he shall nominate, and by and with the Advice and Consent of the Senate, shall appoint Ambassadors, other public Ministers and Consuls, Judges of the supreme Court, and all other Officers of the United States, whose Appointments are not herein otherwise provided for, and which shall be established by Law: but the Congress may by Law vest the Appointment of such inferior Officers, as they think proper, in the President alone, in the Courts of Law, or in the Heads of Departments.

The President shall have Power to fill up all Vacancies that may happen during the Recess of the Senate, by granting Commissions which shall expire at the End of their next Session.

Section 3. He shall from time to time give to the Congress Information of the State of the Union, and recommend to their Consideration such Measures as he shall judge necessary and expedient; he may, on extraordinary Occasions, convene both Houses, or either of them, and in Case of Disagreement between them, with Respect to the Time of Adjournment, he may adjourn them to such Time as he shall think proper; he shall receive Ambassadors and other public Ministers; he shall take Care that the Laws be faithfully executed, and shall Commission all the Officers of the United States.

Section 4. The President, Vice President and all civil Officers of the United States, shall be removed from Office on Impeachment for, and Conviction of, Treason, Bribery, or other high Crimes and Misdemeanors.

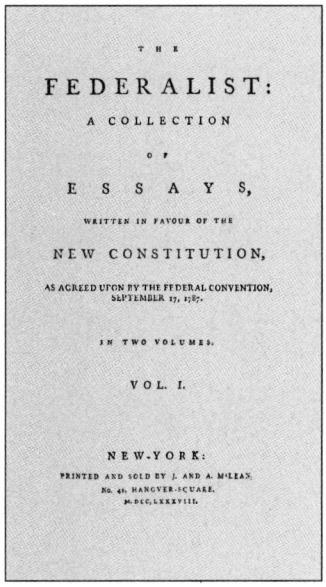
THE
FEDERALIST:
A COLLECTION
OF
ESSAYS,
WRITTEN IN FAVOUR OF THE
NEW CONSTITUTION,
AS AGREED UPON BY THE FEDERAL CONVENTION,
SEPTEMBER 17, 1787.
IN TWO VOLUMES.
VOL. I.
NEW-YORK:
PRINTED AND SOLD BY J. AND A. M'LEAN,
No. 41, HANOVER-SQUARE.
M.DCC.LXXXVIII.

One state in which the battle over ratifying the Constitution raged fiercely was New York. Alexander Hamilton and John Jay, both New York lawyers and politicians, joined with James Madison in writing 85 articles in order to persuade voters to approve the new system of government. They sent these as letters to newspapers, which published them in 1787–1788. These articles are called the Federalist Papers.

In his final speech to the delegates, Benjamin Franklin said, "I consent, Sir, to this Constitution, because I expect no better, and because I am not sure that it is not the best."

ARTICLE III.

Section 1. The judicial Power of the United States shall be vested in one Supreme Court, and in such inferior Courts as the Congress may from time to time ordain and establish. The Judges, both of the supreme and inferior Courts, shall hold their Offices during good Behavior, and shall, at stated Times, receive for their Services, a Compensation, which shall not be diminished during their Continuance in Office.

Section 2. The judicial Power shall extend to all Cases, in Law and Equity, arising under this Constitution, the Laws of the United States, and Treaties made, or which shall be made, under their Authority;—to all Cases affecting Ambassadors, other public Ministers and Consuls;—to all Cases of admiralty and maritime Jurisdiction;—to Controversies to which the United States shall be a Party;—to Controversies between two or more States;—between a State and Citizens of another State [Modified by Amendment XI];—between Citizens of different States;—between Citizens of the same State claiming Lands under Grants of different States, and between a State, or the Citizens thereof, and foreign States, Citizens or Subjects.

In all Cases affecting Ambassadors, other public Ministers and Consuls, and those in which a State shall be a Party, the Supreme Court shall have original Jurisdiction. In all the other Cases before mentioned, the Supreme Court shall have appellate Jurisdiction, both as to Law and Fact, with such Exceptions, and under such Regulations as the Congress shall make.

The Trial of all Crimes, except in Cases of Impeachment, shall be by Jury; and such Trial shall be held in the State where the said Crimes shall have been committed; but when not committed within any State, the Trial shall be at such Place or Places as the Congress may by Law have directed.

Section 3. Treason against the United States, shall consist only in levying War against them, or in adhering to their Enemies, giving them Aid and Comfort. No Person shall be convicted of Treason unless on the Testimony of two Witnesses to the same overt Act, or on Confession in open Court.

The Congress shall have Power to declare the Punishment of Treason, but no Attainder of Treason shall work Corruption of Blood, or Forfeiture except during the Life of the Person attainted.

ARTICLE IV.

Section 1. Full Faith and Credit shall be given in each State to the public Acts, Records, and judicial Proceedings of every other State. And the Congress may by general Laws prescribe the Manner in which such Acts, Records and Proceedings shall be proved, and the Effect thereof.

Section 2. The Citizens of each State shall be entitled to all Privileges and Immunities of Citizens in the several States.

A Person charged in any State with Treason, Felony, or other Crime, who shall flee from Justice, and be found in another State, shall on Demand of the executive Authority of the State from which he fled, be delivered up, to be removed to the State having Jurisdiction of the Crime.

No Person held to Service or Labor in one State, under the Laws thereof, escaping into another, shall, in Consequence of any Law or Regulation therein, be discharged from such Service or Labor, but shall be delivered up on Claim of the Party to whom such Service or Labor may be due [Modified by Amendment XIII].

Section 3. New States may be admitted by the Congress into this Union; but no new State shall be formed or erected within the Jurisdiction of any other State; nor any State be formed by the Junction of two or more States, or Parts of States, without the Consent of the Legislatures of the States concerned as well as of the Congress.

The Congress shall have Power to dispose of and make all needful Rules and Regulations respecting the Territory or other Property belonging to the United States; and nothing in this Constitution shall be so construed as to Prejudice any Claims of the United States, or of any particular State.

Section 4. The United States shall guarantee to every State in this Union a Republican Form of Government, and shall protect each of them against Invasion; and on Application of the Legislature, or of the Executive (when the Legislature cannot be convened), against domestic Violence.

ARTICLE V.

The Congress, whenever two thirds of both Houses shall deem it necessary, shall propose Amendments to this

This 1788 cartoon shows the nine states that first ratified the Constitution as pillars supporting the arch of government. The pillars representing Virginia and New York have not yet been erected because these two states had not yet ratified the document.

Constitution, or on the Application of the Legislatures of two thirds of the several States, shall call a Convention for proposing Amendments, which, in either Case, shall be valid to all Intents and Purposes, as Part of this Constitution, when ratified by the Legislatures of three fourths of the several States, or by Conventions in three fourths thereof, as the one or the other Mode of Ratification may be proposed by the Congress; Provided that no Amendment which may be made prior to the Year One thousand eight hundred and eight shall in any Manner affect the first and fourth Clauses in the Ninth Section of the First Article; and that no State, without its Consent, shall be deprived of its equal Suffrage in the Senate [Possibly abrogated by Amendment XVII].

ARTICLE VI.

All Debts contracted and Engagements entered into, before the Adoption of this Constitution, shall be as valid against the United States under this Constitution, as under the Confederation.

This Constitution, and the Laws of the United States which shall be made in Pursuance thereof; and all Treaties made, or which shall be made, under the Authority of the United States, shall be the supreme Law of the Land; and the Judges in every State shall be bound thereby, any Thing in the Constitution or Laws of any State to the Contrary notwithstanding.

The Senators and Representatives before mentioned, and the Members of the several State Legislatures, and all executive and judicial Officers, both of the United States and of the several States, shall be bound by Oath or Affirmation, to support this Constitution; but no religious Test shall ever be required as a Qualification to any Office or public Trust under the United States.

ARTICLE VII.

The Ratification of the Conventions of nine States shall be sufficient for the Establishment of this Constitution between the States so ratifying the Same.

This wood engraving shows the celebration in New York City following the ratification of the federal Constitution. Alexander Hamilton stands on the ship. He has removed his hat to show his respect to George Washington, who stands on top of the fort in downtown New York City.

THE *BILL OF RIGHTS*

AMENDMENT I

Congress shall make no law respecting an establishment of religion, or prohibiting the free exercise thereof; or abridging the freedom of speech, or of the press; or the right of the people peaceably to assemble, and to petition the Government for a redress of grievances.

AMENDMENT II

A well regulated Militia, being necessary to the security of a free State, the right of the people to keep and bear Arms, shall not be infringed.

James Madison had to work hard to get Congress to pass the Bill of Rights. Some members thought protecting these rights was not very important. Others, who opposed a strong national government and hoped to cripple its powers, fought against passage. In the end, however, popular support helped persuade Congress to approve the first 10 amendments.

AMENDMENT III

No Soldier shall, in time of peace, be quartered in any house, without the consent of the Owner, nor in time of war, but in a manner to be prescribed by law.

AMENDMENT IV

The right of the people to be secure in their persons, houses, papers, and effects, against unreasonable searches and seizures, shall not be violated, and no Warrants shall issue, but upon probable cause, supported by Oath or affirmation, and particularly describing the place to be searched, and the persons or things to be seized.

AMENDMENT V

No person shall be held to answer for a capital or otherwise infamous crime, unless on a presentment or indictment of a Grand Jury, except in cases arising in the land or naval forces, or in the Militia, when in actual service in time of War or public danger; nor shall any person be subject for the same offence to be twice put in jeopardy of life or limb; nor shall be compelled in any criminal case to be a witness against himself, nor be deprived of life, liberty, or property, without due process of law; nor shall private property be taken for public use, without just compensation.

AMENDMENT VI

In all criminal prosecutions, the accused shall enjoy the right to a speedy and public trial, by an impartial jury of the State and district wherein the crime shall have been committed, which district shall have been previously ascertained by law, and to be informed of the nature and cause of the accusation; to be confronted with the witnesses against him; to have compulsory process for obtaining witnesses in his favor, and to have the Assistance of Counsel for his defence.

Congress of the United States,

begun and held at the City of New-York, on

Wednesday the Fourth of March, one thousand seven hundred and eighty nine.

THE Conventions of a number of the States, having at the time of their adopting the Constitution, expressed a desire, in order to prevent misconstruction or abuse of its powers, that further declaratory and restrictive clauses should be added; And as extending the ground of public confidence in the Government will best secure the beneficent ends of its institution

RESOLVED by the Senate and House of Representatives of the United States of America, in Congress assembled, two thirds of both Houses concurring, that the following Articles be proposed to the Legislatures of the several States as amendments to the Constitution of the United States, all or any of which Articles, when ratified by three fourths of the said Legislatures, to be valid to all intents and purposes as part of the said Constitution, viz.

ARTICLES in addition to, and amendment of the Constitution of the United States of America, proposed by Congress, and ratified by the Legislatures of the several States, pursuant to the fifth Article of the original Constitution.

Article the first. ... After the first enumeration required by the first Article of the Constitution, there shall be one Representative for every thirty thousand, until the number shall amount to one hundred, after which, the proportion shall be so regulated by Congress, that there shall be not less than one hundred Representatives, nor less than one Representative for every forty thousand persons, until the number of Representatives shall amount to two hundred, after which the proportion shall be so regulated by Congress, that there shall not be less than two hundred Representatives, nor more than one Representative for every fifty thousand persons.

Article the second. ... No law, varying the compensation for the services of the Senators and Representatives, shall take effect, until an election of Representatives shall have intervened.

Article the third. ... Congress shall make no law respecting an establishment of religion, or prohibiting the free exercise thereof; or abridging the freedom of speech, or of the press, or the right of the people peaceably to assemble, and to petition the Government for a redress of grievances.

Article the fourth. ... A well regulated militia, being necessary to the security of a free State, the right of the people to keep and bear arms, shall not be infringed.

Article the fifth. ... No Soldier shall, in time of peace be quartered in any house, without the consent of the owner, nor in time of war, but in a manner to be prescribed by law.

Article the sixth. ... The right of the people to be secure in their persons, houses, papers, and effects, against unreasonable searches and seizures, shall not be violated, and no Warrants shall issue, but upon probable cause, supported by Oath or affirmation, and particularly describing the place to be searched, and the persons or things to be seized.

Article the seventh. ... No person shall be held to answer for a capital, or otherwise infamous crime, unless on a presentment or indictment of a Grand Jury, except in cases arising in the land or naval forces, or in the Militia, when in actual service in time of War or public danger, nor shall any person be subject for the same offence to be twice put in jeopardy of life or limb, nor shall be compelled in any criminal case to be a witness against himself, nor be deprived of life, liberty, or property, without due process of law; nor shall private property be taken for public use, without just compensation.

Article the eighth. ... In all criminal prosecutions, the accused shall enjoy the right to a speedy and public trial, by an impartial jury of the State and district wherein the crime shall have been committed, which district shall have been previously ascertained by law, and to be informed of the nature and cause of the accusation; to be confronted with the witnesses against him; to have compulsory process for obtaining witnesses in his favor, and to have the assistance of Counsel for his defence.

Article the ninth. ... In suits at common law, where the value in controversy shall exceed twenty dollars, the right of trial by jury shall be preserved, and no fact tried by a jury, shall be otherwise re-examined in any Court of the United States, than according to rules of the common law.

Article the tenth. ... Excessive bail shall not be required, nor excessive fines imposed, nor cruel and unusual punishments inflicted.

Article the eleventh. ... The enumeration in the Constitution, of certain rights, shall not be construed to deny or disparage others retained by the people.

Article the twelfth. ... The powers not delegated to the United States by the Constitution, nor prohibited by it to the States, are reserved to the States respectively, or to the people.

ATTEST,

Frederick Augustus Muhlenberg, Speaker of the House of Representatives.

John Adams, Vice President of the United States, and President of the Senate.

John Beckley, Clerk of the House of Representatives.

Sam. A. Otis, Secretary of the Senate.

The Bill of Rights made sure that Americans would have basic rights such as freedom of speech, religion, and the press.

In 1804 the states ratified two more amendments. No more amendments were added for the next 60 years.

In the Bill of Rights, the Tenth Amendment was the only one that did not protect individual rights. Madison included it to calm the many people who still feared that the new government would have too much power over the states.

AMENDMENT VII

In suits at common law, where the value in controversy shall exceed twenty dollars, the right of trial by jury shall be preserved, and no fact tried by a jury, shall be otherwise reexamined in any Court of the United States, than according to the rules of the common law.

AMENDMENT VIII

Excessive bail shall not be required, nor excessive fines imposed, nor cruel and unusual punishments inflicted.

AMENDMENT IX

The enumeration in the Constitution, of certain rights, shall not be construed to deny or disparage others retained by the people.

AMENDMENT X

The powers not delegated to the United States by the Constitution, nor prohibited by it to the States, are reserved to the States respectively, or to the people.

AUTHOR

Most of the 55 delegates to the Constitutional Convention were merchants, planters, and lawyers. Some of the nation's finest leaders were represented, including George Washington, Alexander Hamilton, James Madison, and Benjamin Franklin. Of all the Constitution's framers, or writers, Madison (1751–1836) made the most significant contribution. For this he is called the Father of the Constitution. Advised by Jefferson, he wrote the Bill of Rights during the first term of Congress. He later served as Secretary of State for Jefferson and, in 1809, was elected the fourth president and served two terms.

RESPONSE

A great national debate arose over the ratification of the Constitution during the fall and winter of 1787 and 1788. Many worried about the centralized government having too much power, preferring power to be in the hands of the states. However, on June 21, New Hampshire became the ninth state to ratify it, establishing the Constitution as the law of the land. Within two years, Rhode Island, the remaining state, had ratified it.

Passing the Bill of Rights was slightly difficult as well. Six months after its submission, 9 out of the 10 states needed for approval had ratified. But then everything stalled. For various reasons, Virginia, Georgia, and Connecticut held out. It wasn't until Vermont was admitted to the Union in 1791 that another state ratified the Bill of Rights. Virginia quickly followed Vermont's lead and the Bill of Rights became an essential part of the Constitution.

One of the two amendments the states did not ratify dealt with the number of representatives in Congress. The other amendment that the states refused to approve became the Twenty-seventh Amendment in 1992. This amendment prevents Congress from passing immediate salary increases for itself. It says, "No law varying the compensation for the services of the senators and representatives shall take effect, until an election of representatives shall have intervened."

Farewell Address

(SEPTEMBER 17, 1796)

GEORGE WASHINGTON

Numerous towns, cities, bridges, parks, and monuments have been named for George Washington, not to mention one state and our nation's capital. His image can be found printed on the one dollar bill, engraved on the quarter and the Purple Heart, and carved on Mount Rushmore.

Americans loved, respected, and admired their first president throughout his life, even after his retirement. This portrait of Washington in his old age captures his directness and dignity.

At the end of two terms, a weary George Washington decided to retire from the office of President of the United States. In his Farewell Address, he appealed for national unity, warning against sectional loyalty. Alarmed by the bitter rivalry between the two political parties, Federalists and Republicans, he cautioned against political strife. In the second, and most famous, part of his address, he urged the United States to develop its foreign trade but make no permanent alliances with other nations. This advice guided United States foreign policy until the twentieth century.

The period for a new election of a citizen to administer the executive government of the United States being not far distant, and the time actually arrived when your thoughts must be employed in designating the person who is to be clothed with that important trust, it appears to me proper, especially as it may conduce to a more distinct expression of the public voice, that I should now apprise you of the resolution I have formed to decline being considered among the number of those out of whom a choice is to be made. . . .

The unity of government which constitutes you one people is also now dear to you. It is justly so, for it is a main pillar in the edifice of your real independence, the support of your tranquility at home, your peace abroad, of your safety, of your prosperity, of that very liberty which you so highly prize. But as it is easy to foresee that from different causes and from different quarters much pains will be taken, many artifices employed, to weaken in your minds the conviction of this truth, as this is the point in your political fortress against which the batteries of internal and external enemies will be most constantly and actively (though often covertly and insidiously) directed, it is of infinite moment that you should properly estimate the immense value of your national union to your collective and individual happiness; that you should cherish a cordial, habitual, and immovable attachment to it; accustoming yourselves to think and speak of it as of the palladium of your political safety and prosperity; watching for its preservation with jealous anxiety; discountenancing whatever may suggest even a suspicion that it can in any event be abandoned, and indignantly frowning upon the first dawning of every attempt to alienate any portion of our country from the rest or to enfeeble the sacred ties which now link together the various parts.

For this you have every inducement of sympathy and interest. Citizens by birth or choice of a common country, that country has a right to concentrate your affections. The name of American, which belongs to you in your national capacity, must always exalt the just pride of patriotism more than any appellation derived from local discriminations. With slight shades of difference, you have the same religion, manners, habits, and political principles. You have in a common cause fought and

After completing two terms as president, Washington wanted to retire. He refused to be considered for a third term and returned home to Virginia to his beloved plantation, Mount Vernon. It had been his home for 45 years and Washington took great pride in the land and buildings.

Official presidential residences were not provided for the nation's earliest leaders. The first presidential mansion was Washington's home in New York City—No. 1 Cherry Street—where he lived from 1789 to 1790.

triumphed together. The independence and liberty you possess are the work of joint councils and joint efforts, of common dangers, sufferings, and successes. . . .

In contemplating the causes which may disturb our union it occurs as matter of serious concern that any ground should have been furnished for characterizing parties by geographical discriminations—*Northern* and *Southern*, *Atlantic* and *Western*—whence designing men may endeavor to excite a belief that there is a real difference of local interests and views. One of the expedients of party to acquire influence within particular districts is to misrepresent the opinions and aims of other districts. You can not shield yourselves too much against the jealousies and heartburnings which spring from these misrepresentations; they tend to render alien to each other those who ought to be bound together by fraternal affection. . . .

To the efficacy and permanency of your union a government for the whole is indispensable. No alliances, however strict, between the parts can be an adequate substitute. They must inevitably experience the infractions and interruptions which all alliances in all times have experienced. Sensible of this momentous truth, you have improved upon your first essay by the adoption of a Constitution of government better calculated than your former for an intimate union and for the efficacious management of your common concerns. This government, the offspring of our own choice, uninfluenced and unawed, adopted upon full investigation and mature deliberation, completely free in its principles, in the distribution of its powers, uniting security with energy, and containing within itself a provision for its own amendment, has a just claim to your confidence and your support. Respect for its authority, compliance with its laws, acquiescence in its measures, are duties enjoined by the fundamental maxims of true liberty. The basis of our political systems is the right of the people to make and to alter their constitutions of government. But the constitution which at any time exists till changed by an explicit and authentic act of the whole people is sacredly obligatory upon all. The very idea of the power and the right of the people to establish government presupposes the duty of every individual to obey the established government. . . .

Toward the preservation of your government and the permanency of your present happy state, it is requisite not only that you steadily discountenance irregular oppositions to its acknowledged authority, but also that you resist with care the spirit of innovation upon its principles, however specious the pretexts. One method of assault may be to effect in the forms of the Constitution alterations which will impair the energy of the system, and thus to undermine what can not be directly overthrown. In all the changes to which you may be invited remember that time and habit are at least as necessary to fix the true character of governments as of other human institutions; that experience is the surest standard by which to test the real tendency of the existing constitution of a country; that facility in changes upon the credit of mere hypothesis and opinion exposes to perpetual change, from the endless variety of hypothesis and opinion; and remember especially that for the efficient management of your common interests in a country so extensive as ours a government of as much vigor as is consistent with the perfect security of liberty is indispensable. . . .

I have already intimated to you the danger of parties in the state, with particular reference to the founding of them on geographical discriminations. Let me now take a more comprehensive view, and warn you in the most solemn manner against the baneful effects of the spirit of party generally.

This spirit, unfortunately, is inseparable from our nature, having its root in the strongest passions of the human mind. It exists under different shapes in all governments, more or less stifled, controlled, or repressed; but in those of the popular form it is seen in its greatest rankness and is truly their worst enemy. . . .

It serves always to distract the public councils and enfeeble the public administration. It agitates the community with illfounded jealousies and false alarms; kindles the animosity of one part against another; foments occasionally riot and insurrection. It opens the door to foreign influence and corruption, which find a facilitated access to the government itself through the channels of party passion. Thus the policy and the will of one country are subjected to the policy and will of another. . . .

George Washington delivered the Farewell Address to his cabinet, and it was published in the newspapers the next day.

Of all the dispositions and habits which lead to political prosperity, religion and morality are indispensable supports. In vain would that man claim the tribute of patriotism who should labor to subvert these great pillars of human happiness—these firmest props of the duties of men and citizens. The mere politician, equally with the pious man, ought to respect and to cherish them. A volume could not trace all their connections with private and public felicity. Let it simply be asked, Where is the security for property, for reputation, for life, if the sense of religious obligation desert the oaths which are the instruments of investigation in courts of justice? And let us with caution indulge the supposition that morality can be maintained without religion. Whatever may be conceded to the influence of refined education on minds of peculiar structure, reason and experience both forbid us to expect that national morality can prevail in exclusion of religious principle.

It is substantially true that virtue or morality is a necessary spring of popular government. The rule indeed extends with more or less force to every species of free government. Who that is a sincere friend to it can look with indifference upon attempts to shake the foundation of the fabric? Promote, then, as an object of primary importance, institutions for the general diffusion of knowledge. In proportion as the structure of a government gives force to public opinion, it is essential that public opinion should be enlightened.

As a very important source of strength and security, cherish public credit. One method of preserving it is to use it as sparingly as possible, avoiding occasions of expense by cultivating peace, but remembering also that timely disbursements to prepare for danger frequently prevent much greater disbursements to repel it; avoiding likewise the accumulation of debt, not only by shunning of expense, but by vigorous exertions in time of peace to discharge the debts which unavoidable wars have occasioned, not ungenerously throwing upon prosperity the burden which we ourselves ought to bear. . . .

Against the insidious wiles of foreign influence (I conjure you to believe me, fellow-citizens) the jealousy of a free people ought to be *constantly* awake, since history and experience prove that foreign influence is one of the most baneful foes of

The whole country was saddened by Washington's death on December, 14, 1798. Cavalry general Henry Lee delivered the funeral oration. He said that Washington was "First in war, first in peace and first in the hearts of his countrymen. . . ."

republican government. But that jealousy, to be useful, must be impartial, else it becomes the instrument of the very influence to be avoided, instead of a defense against it. Excessive partiality for one foreign nation and excessive dislike of another cause those whom that actuate to see danger only on one side, and serve to veil and even second the arts of influence on the other. Real patriots who may resist the intrigues of the favorite are liable to become suspected and odious, while its tools and dupes usurp the applause and confidence of the people to surrender their interests.

The great rule of conduct for us in regard to foreign nations is, in extending our commercial relations to have with them as little *political* connection as possible. So far as we have already formed engagements let them be fulfilled with perfect good faith. Here let us stop.

Europe has a set of primary interests which to us have none or a very remote relation. Hence she must be engaged in frequent controversies, the causes of which are essentially foreign to our concerns. Hence, therefore, it must be unwise in us to implicate ourselves to artificial ties in the ordinary vicissitudes of her politics or the ordinary combinations and collisions of her friendships or enmities.

Our detached and distant situation invites and enables us to pursue a different course. If we remain one people, under an efficient government, the period is not far off when we may defy material injury from external annoyance; when we may take such an attitude as will cause the neutrality we may at any time resolve upon to be scrupulously respected; when belligerent nations, under the impossibility of making acquisitions upon us, will not lightly hazard the giving us provocation; when we may choose peace or war, as our interest, guided by justice, shall counsel.

Why forego the advantages of so peculiar a situation? Why quit our own to stand upon foreign ground? Why, by interweaving our destiny with that of any part of Europe, entangle our peace and prosperity in the toils of European ambition, rivalship, interest, humor, or caprice?. . .

Though in reviewing the incidents of my administration I am unconscious of intentional error, I am nevertheless too sen-

The president was exhausted by attacks of the Republican-Democrats, who were led by Thomas Jefferson. Angry at Washington's support of the Federalists, the Republican-Democrats, or Republicans, no longer referred to him as the "father of the country." Rather, they called him the "stepfather of his country."

Washington's warning against "entangling alliances" with other nations became known as the "Great Rule." The "Great Rule" guided American foreign policy until 1917, when the United States declared war against Germany. In entering World War I, America allied herself with three great European powers—Britain, France, and Russia.

sible of my defects not to think it probable that I may have committed many errors. Whatever they may be, I fervently beseech the Almighty to avert or mitigate the evils to which they may tend. I shall also carry with me the hope that my country will never cease to view them with indulgence, and that, after forty-five years of my life dedicated to its service with an upright zeal, the faults of incompetent abilities will be consigned to oblivion, as myself must soon be to the mansions of rest.

Relying on its kindness in this as in other things, and actuated by that fervent love toward it which is so natural to a man who views in it the native soil of himself and his progenitors for several generations, I anticipate with pleasing expectation that retreat in which I promise myself to realize without alloy the sweet enjoyment of partaking in the midst of my fellow citizens the benign influence of good laws under a free government—the ever-favorite object of my heart, and the happy reward, as I trust, of our mutual cares, labors, and dangers.

The nation's first president, George Washington, says an emotional farewell to his officers at the end of his presidency.

AUTHOR

George Washington (1732–1799) had reluctantly agreed to a second term as the nation's first president. By its end, he was longing to return to private life. So he firmly rejected the offer of a third term. James Madison wrote a first draft of this farewell address. Secretary of the Treasury Alexander Hamilton then helped the president revise the document.

RESPONSE

Washington hoped his address would reduce political fighting, but the two parties ignored his warnings. By the end of the 1796 presidential campaign, political passions had flared as hot as ever. Many Republicans and Federalists were not even speaking to each other. John Adams succeeded Washington as president.

George Washington's wife, Martha, was not entirely comfortable in the role of first lady. Though she entertained often and was a hospitable hostess, she longed to return to Mount Vernon, away from the public life. While Washington was president, Martha wrote to a niece, confiding in her that she would "much rather be at home."

THE STAR-SPANGLED BANNER

(SEPTEMBER 16, 1814)

FRANCIS SCOTT KEY

Francis Scott Key's poem "The Star-Spangled Banner" was adopted as the United States's national anthem in 1931.

Francis Scott Key wrote "The Star-Spangled Banner" during the War of 1812 between England and the United States. In September 1814, English troops entered Washington, D.C., and set fire to most of the government buildings. During their withdrawal from the city, they captured a friend of Key's. Soon afterward, Key and a government official sailed to the British fleet in Maryland's Chesapeake Bay to try to negotiate his friend's release. The British agreed to let the man go, but they were about to attack Baltimore and detained the Americans until after the attack. So Key and the government official sailed with the British, and, on September 13, they watched them fire on Fort McHenry, near Baltimore's harbor.

The bombardment lasted most of the night. At dawn, Key was overjoyed to see the fort was still flying the American flag. He began scribbling a few lines describing the bombardment. After Key returned to Baltimore, he completed his song.

Oh, say, can you see, by the dawn's early light,
What so proudly we hailed at the twilight's last gleaming,
Whose broad stripes and bright stars through the perilous fight,
O'er the ramparts we watched were so gallantly streaming?
And the rockets' red glare, the bombs bursting in air,
Gave proof thro' the night that our flag was still there.
Oh, say, does that star-spangled banner yet wave
O'er the land of the free, and the home of the brave!

On the shore, dimly seen thro' the mists of the deep,
Where the foe's haughty host in dread silence reposes,
What is that which the breeze o'er the towering steep,
As it fitfully blows, half conceals, half discloses?
Now it catches the gleam of the morning's first beam,
In full glory reflected, now shines on the stream.
'Tis the star-spangled banner; oh, long may it wave
O'er the land of the free, and the home of the brave!

And where is that band who so vauntingly swore
That the havoc of war and the battle's confusion
A home and a country should leave us no more?

The flag that Key saw flying over Fort McHenry covers one wall of the Smithsonian Institution's Museum of American History in Washington, D.C.

The people of Baltimore quickly began singing Key's words, to the popular British tune, "To Anacreon in Heaven."

Their blood has washed out their foul
footsteps' pollution.
No refuge could save the hireling and slave
From the terror of flight, or the gloom of the
grave:
And the star-spangled banner in triumph doth
wave
O'er the land of the free, and the home of the
brave!

Oh, thus be it ever when freemen shall stand
Between their loved homes and the war's
desolation;
Blest with victory and peace, may the heaven-
rescued land
Praise the power that hath made and
preserved us a nation!
Then conquer we must, when our cause it is
just,
And this be our motto: "In God is our trust!"
And the star-spangled banner in triumph doth
wave,
O'er the land of the free, and the home of the
brave!

On January 8, 1815, Americans led by General Andrew Jackson (shown raising his sword in victory) defeated the British at the Battle of New Orleans. Jackson thought the battle ended the War of 1812, but the United States and Great Britain had signed a peace treaty a few days earlier in Europe. The armies gathered at New Orleans did not receive news of the peace treaty until after the battle.

This view of the bombardment of Fort McHenry shows the "bombs bursting in air" that Key described in "The Star-Spangled Banner."

AUTHOR

Born to a prosperous Maryland family, Francis Scott Key (1779–1843) was a well-known lawyer. He served as district attorney for the District of Columbia from 1833 to 1841. Key was also a founder of the American Colonization Society. This organization attempted to end slavery by returning freed slaves to Africa. Key kept writing poetry as a hobby throughout his life.

RESPONSE

Several days after the bombardment, Key's poem, "Defence of Fort McHenry," appeared on printed notices and was circulated around Baltimore. Soon it was published under the title "The Star-Spangled Banner." Shortly afterward, it became popular in other American cities.

THE MONROE DOCTRINE

(DECEMBER 2, 1823)

JAMES MONROE

James Monroe was experienced in foreign policy before he became president, serving as ambassador to France, England, and Spain. As ambassador to France during Jefferson's administration, Monroe had helped arrange for the Louisiana Purchase.

President James Monroe outlined what is now known as the Monroe Doctrine in a speech to Congress. The president warned European nations not to interfere in the affairs of America's neighbors—the nations of the Western Hemisphere. Monroe was responding to European threats to aid Spain in regaining its former Latin American colonies. By 1822, Argentina, Columbia, and Mexico had revolted and declared their independence.

Monroe's brief statement has guided much of American policy in Latin America. Originally, the doctrine had been intended to support weak Latin American countries against great powers and discourage Russian interference along the Pacific Northwest Coast. But the United States gradually used it to defend its own interference in Latin America, so many nations to the south grew resentful. In the late 1920s the United States decided on a new approach and began offering economic assistance to and cooperation with its Latin American neighbors.

. . . At the proposal of the Russian Imperial Government, made through the minister of the Emperor residing here, a full power and instructions have been transmitted to the minister of the United States at St. Petersburg to arrange by amicable negotiation the respective rights and interests of the two nations on the northwest coast of this continent. A similar proposal had been made by his Imperial Majesty to the Government of Great Britain, which has likewise been acceded to. The Government of the United States has been desirous by this friendly proceeding of manifesting the great value which they have invariably attached to the friendship of the Emperor and their solicitude to cultivate the best understanding with his Government. In the discussions to which this interest has given rise and in the arrangements by which they may terminate, the occasion has been judged proper for asserting, as a principle in which the rights and interests of the United States are involved, that the American continents, by the free and independent condition which they have assumed and maintain, are henceforth not to be considered as subjects for future colonization by any Europeans powers. . . .

. . . In the wars of the European powers in matters relating to themselves we have never taken any part, nor does it comport with our policy so to do. It is only when our rights are invaded or seriously menaced that we resent injuries or make preparation for our defense. With the movements in this hemisphere we are of necessity more immediately connected, and by causes which must be obvious to all enlightened and impartial observers. The political system of the allied powers is essentially different in this respect from that of America. This difference proceeds from that which exists in their respective Governments; and between those new Governments and Spain we declared our neutrality at the time of their recognition, and to this we have adhered, and shall continue to adhere, provided no change shall occur which, in the judgment of the competent authorities of this Government, shall make a corresponding change on the part of the United States indispensable to their security.

The late events in Spain and Portugal show that Europe is still unsettled. Of this important fact no stronger proof can be

The Monroe Doctrine was part of the president's annual message to Congress.

adduced than that the allied powers should have thought it proper, on any principle satisfactory to themselves, to have interposed by force in the internal concerns of Spain. To what extent such interposition may be carried, on the same principle, is a question in which all independent powers whose governments differ from theirs are interested, even those most remote, and surely none more so than the United States. Our policy in regard to Europe, which was adopted at an early stage of the wars which have so long agitated that quarter of the globe, nevertheless remains the same, which is, not to interfere in the internal concerns of any of its powers; to consider the government de facto as the legitimate government for us; to cultivate friendly relations with it, and to preserve those relations by a frank, firm, and manly policy, meeting in all instances the just claims of every power, submitting to injuries from none. But in regard to those continents circumstances are eminently and conspicuously different. It is impossible that the allied powers should extend their political system to any portion of either continent without endangering our peace and happiness; nor can anyone believe that our southern brethren, if left to themselves, would adopt it of their own accord. It is equally impossible, therefore, that we should behold such interposition in any form with indifference. If we look to the comparative strength and resources of Spain and those new Governments, and their distance from each other, it must be obvious that she can never subdue them. It is still the true policy of the United States to leave the parties to themselves, in the hope that other powers will pursue the same course. . . .

In 1842 President John Tyler used this document to justify taking Texas from Mexico. A Venezuelan newspaper then warned other Latin American countries against the United States: "Beware, brother, the wolf approaches the lambs."

AUTHOR

James Monroe (1758–1831) was the fifth president of the United States (1817–1825). The last of the founding fathers to serve as president, he was an excellent administrator. During Monroe's second term, Secretary of State John Quincy Adams (1767–1848) did not want to make enemies of the European powers, but he also did not want the foreign policy of the United States to be controlled by them. With this in mind, Adams drafted a new American policy for the Western Hemisphere that later became known as the Monroe Doctrine.

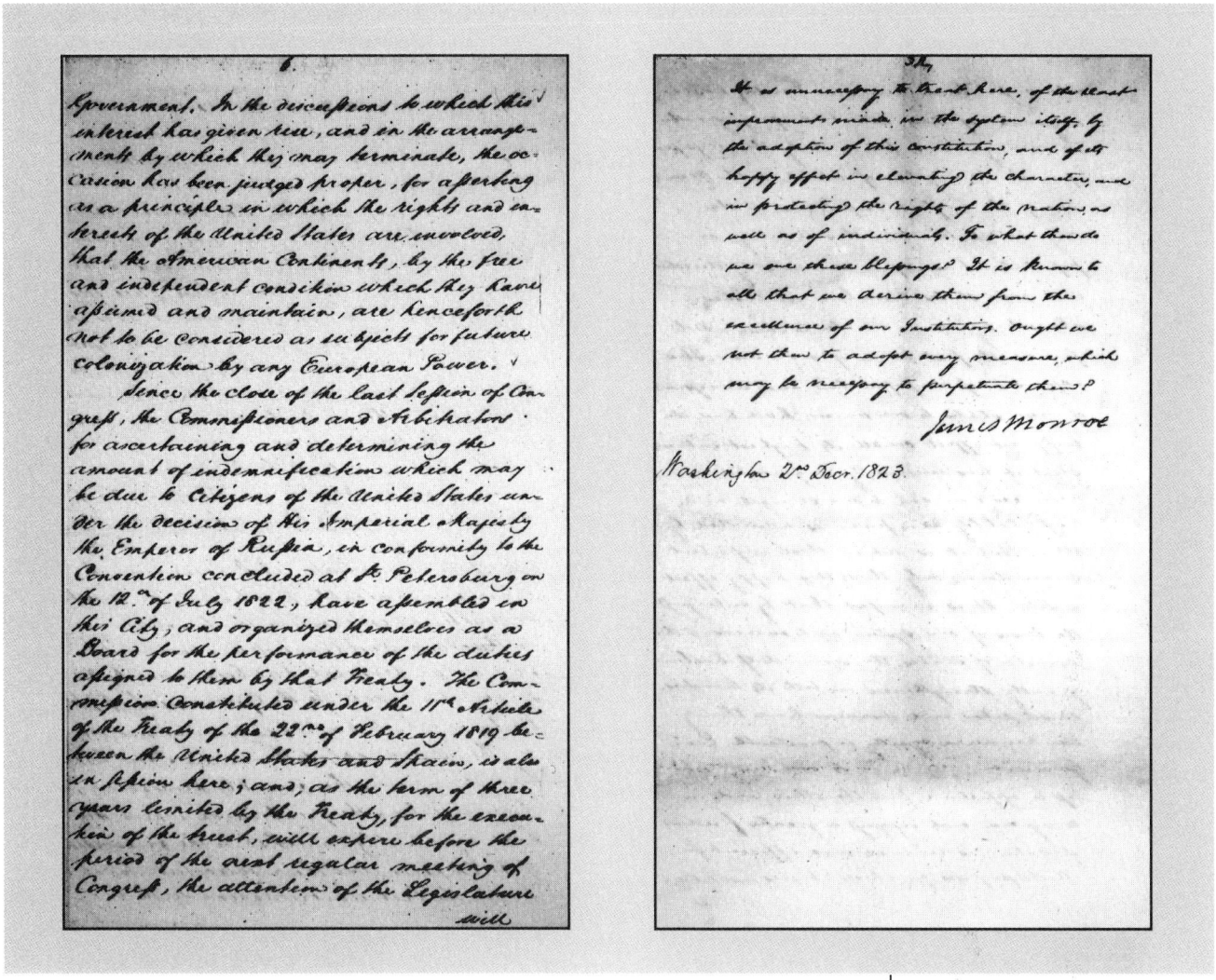

6.

Government. In the discussions to which this interest has given rise, and in the arrangements by which they may terminate, the occasion has been judged proper, for asserting as a principle in which the rights and interests of the United States are involved, that the American Continents, by the free and independent condition which they have assumed and maintain, are henceforth not to be considered as subjects for future colonization by any European Power.

Since the close of the last session of Congress, the Commissioners and Arbitrators for ascertaining and determining the amount of indemnification which may be due to Citizens of the United States under the decision of His Imperial Majesty the Emperor of Russia, in conformity to the Convention concluded at St. Petersburg on the 12th of July 1822, have assembled in this City, and organized themselves as a Board for the performance of the duties assigned to them by that Treaty. The Commission constituted under the 11th Article of the Treaty of the 22nd of February 1819 between the United States and Spain, is also in session here; and, as the term of three years limited by the Treaty, for the execution of the trust, will expire before the period of the next regular meeting of Congress, the attention of the Legislature will

34

be as unnecessary to dwell here, of the utmost importance minds in the system itself, by the adoption of this constitution, and of its happy effect in elevating the character, and in protecting the rights of the nation, as well as of individuals. To what shall we owe these blessings? It is known to all that we derive them from the excellence of our Institutions. Ought we not then to adopt every measure, which may be necessary to perpetuate them?

James Monroe

Washington 2d Decr. 1823.

A photograph from the National Archives shows pages 6 and 34 of Monroe's message to Congress, part of which became known as the Monroe Doctrine. England's support of the doctrine helped keep Europe's other great powers out of Latin America. The reason was simple: No European nation wanted to take on Britain's powerful navy.

RESPONSE

The American people praised Monroe's statement. But the European powers did not take Monroe's warning seriously. In 1823 the United States was not a world power. It lacked the military strength to keep European countries out of Latin America.

Declaration of Sentiments

SENECA FALLS CONVENTION

(JULY 20, 1848)

Elizabeth Cady Stanton was photographed with her eldest child, Daniel, in 1854. As a child Stanton spent time at her father's law practice. Several times she heard him explaining to women the laws that did not allow them to own property.

In 1848 American women had almost no legal rights. They could not own property or gain custody of their children in a divorce. They did not even have the right to vote. Two women, Lucretia Mott and Elizabeth Cady Stanton, organized a convention to discuss women's issues. Nearly three hundred people, mostly women, attended the meeting at Seneca Falls, New York, on July 19 and 20. There, they debated and adopted a "Declaration of Sentiments," which was deliberately modeled on the Declaration of Independence.

The Seneca Falls Convention was the first women's rights meeting in the United States. The Declaration of Sentiments launched the modern movement for gender equality. Feminists fought from then on to gain for women the same political, social, and legal rights enjoyed by men.

When, in the course of human events, it becomes necessary for one portion of the family of man to assume among the people of the earth a position different from that which they have hitherto occupied, but one to which the laws of nature and of nature's God entitle them, a decent respect to the opinions of mankind requires that they should declare the causes that impel them to such a course.

We hold these truths to be self-evident: that all men and women are created equal; that they are endowed by their Creator with certain inalienable rights; that among these are life, liberty, and the pursuit of happiness; that to secure these rights governments are instituted, deriving their just powers from the consent of the governed. Whenever any form of government becomes destructive of these ends, it is the right of those who suffer from it to refuse allegiance to it, and to insist upon the institution of a new government, laying its foundation on such principles, and organizing its powers in such form, as to them shall seem most likely to effect their safety and happiness. Prudence, indeed, will dictate that governments long established should not be changed for light and transient causes; and accordingly all experience hath shown that mankind are more disposed to suffer, while evils are sufferable, than to right themselves by abolishing the forms to which they are accustomed. But when a long train of abuses and usurpations, pursing invariably the same object evinces a design to reduce them under absolute despotism, it is their duty to throw off such government, and to provide new guards for their future security. Such has been the patient sufferance of the women under this government, and such is now the necessity which constrains them to demand the equal station to which they are entitled.

The history of mankind is a history of repeated injuries and usurpations on the part of man toward woman, having in direct object the establishment of an absolute tyranny over her. To prove this, let facts be submitted to a candid world.

He has never permitted her to exercise her inalienable right to the elective franchise.

He has compelled her to submit to laws, in the formation of which she had no voice.

He has withheld from her rights which are given to the most

A woman who attended the convention recalled, "At first we travelled quite alone. But before we had gone many miles we came on other wagon-loads of women, bound in the same direction."

ignorant and degraded men—both natives and foreigners.

Having deprived her of this first right of a citizen, the elective franchise, thereby leaving her without representation in the halls of legislation, he has oppressed her on all sides.

He has made her, if married, in the eye of the law, civilly dead.

He has taken from her all right in property, even to the wages she earns.

He has made her, morally, an irresponsible being, as she can commit many crimes with impunity, provided they be done in the presence of her husband. In the covenant of marriage, she is compelled to promise obedience to her husband, he becoming, to all intents and purposes, her master—the law giving him power to deprive her of her liberty, and to administer chastisement.

He has so framed the laws of divorce, as to what shall be the proper causes and in case of separation, to whom the guardianship of the children shall be given, as to be wholly regardless of the happiness of women—the law, in all cases, going upon a false supposition of the supremacy of man, and giving all power into his hands.

After depriving her of all rights as a married woman, if single, and the owner of property, he has taxed her to support a government which recognizes her only when her property can be made profitable to it.

He has monopolized nearly all the profitable employments, and from those she is permitted to follow, she receives but a scanty remuneration. He closes against her all the avenues to wealth and distinction which he considers most honorable to himself. As a teacher of theology, medicine, or law, she is not known.

He has denied her the facilities for obtaining a thorough education, all colleges being closed against her.

He allows her in Church, as well as State, but a subordinate position, claiming Apostolic authority for her exclusion from the ministry, and, with some exceptions, from any public participation in the affairs of the Church.

He has created a false public sentiment by giving to the world a different code of morals for men and women, by which

The few men who participated in the convention were abolitionists. Abolitionists were people who worked for the immediate end, or abolition, of slavery in the United States. They also condemned racial prejudice. Women's rights were not their primary focus.

moral delinquencies which exclude women from society, are not only tolerated, but deemed of little account in man.

He has usurped the prerogative of Jehovah himself, claiming it as his right to assign for her a sphere of action, when that belongs to her conscience and to her God.

He has endeavored, in every way that he could, to destroy her confidence in her own powers, to lessen her self-respect and to make her willing to lead a dependent and abject life.

Now, in view of this entire disfranchisement of one-half the people of this country, their social and religious degradation—in view of the unjust laws above mentioned, and because women do feel themselves aggrieved, oppressed, and fraudulently deprived of their most sacred rights, we insist that they have immediate admission to all the rights and privileges which belong to them as citizens of the United States.

In entering upon the great work before us, we anticipate no small amount of misconception, misrepresentation, and ridicule; but we shall use every instrumentality within our power to effect our object. We shall employ agents, circulate tracts, petition the State and National legislatures, and endeavor to enlist the pulpit and the press in our behalf. We hope this Convention will be followed by a series of Conventions embracing every part of the country.

Firmly relying upon the final triumph of the Right and the True, we do this day affix our signatures to this declaration. . . .

Resolved, That such laws as conflict, in any way, with the true and substantial happiness of woman, are contrary to the great precept of nature, and of no validity; for this is "superior in obligation to any other."

Resolved, That all laws which prevent woman from occupying such a station in society as her conscience shall dictate, or which place her in a position inferior to that of man, are contrary to the great precept of nature, and therefore of no force or authority.

Resolved, That woman is man's equal—was intended to be so by the Creator, and the highest good of the race demands that she should be recognized as such.

Resolved, That the women of this country ought to be enlightened in regard to the laws under which they live, that

This illustration shows Elizabeth Cady Stanton addressing the Seneca Falls Convention in 1848. In the 1840s respectable women did not speak in public, and calling a meeting was almost unheard of. Stanton said later, "We felt helpless and hopeless, as if we had suddenly been asked to construct a steam engine."

Susan B. Anthony, another advocate of women's rights, seated in her office in 1900. The photographs on Anthony's desk are of the many women who fought to promote woman suffrage. On a visit to Seneca Falls, three years after the convention, Anthony first met Elizabeth Cady Stanton. The two joined forces to lead the feminist movement for the next 50 years.

they may no longer publish their degradation by declaring themselves satisfied with their present position, nor their ignorance, by asserting that they have all the rights they want.

Resolved, That inasmuch as man, while claiming for himself intellectual superiority, does accord to woman moral superiority, it is pre-eminently his duty to encourage her to speak and teach, as she has an opportunity, in all religious assemblies.

Resolved, That the same amount of virtue, delicacy, and refinement of behavior that is required of woman in the social state, should also be required of man, and the same transgressions should be visited with equal severity on both man and woman.

Resolved, That the objection of indelicacy and impropriety, which is so often brought against woman when she addresses a public audience, comes with a very ill-grace from those who encourage, by their attendance, her appearance on the stage, in the concert, or in feats of the circus.

Resolved, That woman has too long rested satisfied in the circumscribed limits which corrupt customs and a perverted application of the Scriptures have marked out for her, and that it is time she should move in the enlarged sphere which her great Creator has assigned her.

Resolved, That it is the duty of the women of this country to secure to themselves their sacred right to the elective franchise.

Resolved, That the equality of human rights results necessarily from the fact of the identity of the race in capabilities and responsibilities.

Resolved, That the speedy success of our cause depends upon the zealous and untiring efforts of both men and women, for the overthrow of the monopoly of the pulpit, and for the securing to women an equal participation with men in the various trades, professions, and commerce.

Resolved, therefore, That, being invested by the Creator with the same capabilities, and the same consciousness of responsibility for their exercise, it is demonstrably the right and duty of woman, equally with man, to promote every righteous cause by every righteous means; and especially in regard to the great subjects of morals and religion, it is self-evidently her right to participate with her brother in teaching them, both in private and in public, by writing and by speaking, by any instrumentalities proper to be used, and in any assemblies proper to be held; and this being a self-evident truth growing out of the divinely implanted principles of human nature, any custom or authority adverse to it, whether modern or wearing the hoary sanction of antiquity, is to be regarded as self-evident falsehood, and at war with the interests of mankind.

During the Seneca Falls Convention, Elizabeth Cady Stanton introduced the resolution demanding that women have the right to vote. The resolution was approved. But because the idea of women voting was so far ahead of its time, it was the only resolution that did not pass unanimously. American women finally won the vote in 1920, with the passing of the Ninteenth Amendment to the Constitution.

AUTHORS

The Declaration of Sentiments represented the combined efforts of the women and men attending the convention. However, Lucretia Mott (1793–1880) and Elizabeth Cady Stanton (1815–1902) played key roles. Mott was an abolitionist and a feminist. She went to London in 1840 for the World's Anti-Slavery Convention, but became infuriated when she was not allowed to attend because she was a woman. While in London she met Elizabeth Cady Stanton, who had also traveled there for the convention. Influenced by Mott, Stanton went on to become a leader of the women's rights movement. In 1869 Stanton helped found the first organization to push for a constitutional amendment giving women the right to vote.

RESPONSE

Most Americans in the mid-nineteenth century did not believe that women should have the same rights as men. So it was not surprising that the newspapers that reported the convention made fun of it. But the participants felt their meeting was a success, so they planned a second meeting three weeks later in Rochester, New York.

Uncle Tom's Cabin

(1852)

Harriet Beecher Stowe

Harriet Beecher Stowe had never witnessed slavery in the Deep South, but she had seen it during a visit to Kentucky. Stowe had also lived for many years in Ohio, a free state bordered by slave states.

The novel *Uncle Tom's Cabin* was the most popular piece of antislavery writing before the Civil War. Harriet Beecher Stowe, a white woman, was the author. The novel told the story of Uncle Tom, a black slave, who was harshly treated by Simon Legree, a cruel white overseer. Stowe's novel increased the tensions between the North and the South before the Civil War. The following description of a slave auction is from Chapter 12, "Select Incident of Lawful Trade."

This engraving from the novel Uncle Tom's Cabin *illustrates the sad separation of Hagar and her son Albert. "The old men of the company, partly by persuasion and partly by force, loosed the poor creature's last despairing hold, and, as they led her off to her new master's waggon, strove to comfort her."*

. . . The men and women to be sold sat in a group apart, talking in a low tone to each other. The woman who had been advertised by the name of Hagar was a regular African in feature and figure. She might have been sixty, but was older than that by hard work and disease, was partially blind and somewhat crippled with rheumatism. By her side stood her only remaining son, Albert, a bright-looking little fellow of fourteen years. The boy was the only survivor of a large family, who had been successively sold away from her to a southern market. The mother held on to him with both her shaking hands, and eyed with intense trepidation every one who walked up to examine him.

"Don't be fear'd, Aunt Hagar," said the oldest of the men. "I spoke to Mas'r Thomas 'bout it, and he thought he might manage to sell you in a lot both together."

"Dey needn't call me worn out yet," said she, lifting her shaking hands. "I can cook yet, and scrub, and scour,—I'm wuth a buying, if I do come cheap; tell 'em dat ar—you *tell* 'em," she added, earnestly.

Haley here forced his way into the group, walked up to the. . . man, pulled his mouth open and looked in, felt of his teeth, made him stand and straighten himself, bend his back, and perform various evolutions, to show his muscles; and then passed on to the next, and put him through the same trial. Walking up last to the boy, he felt of his arms, straightened his hands, and looked at his fingers, and made him jump, to show his agility.

"He an't gwine to be sold widout me!" said the old woman, with passionate eagerness; "he and I goes in a lot together. I's rail strong yet, Mas'r, and can do heaps o' work—heaps on it, Mas'r." . . .

"What think of 'em?" said a man who had been following Haley's examination, as if to make up his own mind from it.

"Wal," said Haley, spitting. "I shall put in, I think, for the youngerly ones and the boy."

"They want to sell the boy and the old woman together," said the man.

"Find it a tight pull,—Why, she's an old rack o' bones—not worth her salt!"

Harriet Beecher Stowe wrote Uncle Tom's Cabin *at the kitchen table in the evenings after her eight children were asleep.*

The novel was turned into a play in the 1850s. Uncle Tom's Cabin *became one of the most popular plays in the second half of the nineteenth century.*

"You wouldn't, then?" said the man.

"Anybody'd be a fool 't would. She's half-blind, crooked with rheumatis, and foolish to boot.". . .

"No go, 't all," said Haley, "wouldn't take her for a present—fact, I've seen, now."

"Wal, 'tis kinder pity, now, not to buy her with her son—her heart seems so sot on him,—s'pose they fling her in cheap."

"Them that's got money to spend that ar way, it's all well enough. I shall bid off on that ar boy for a plantation hand;—wouldn't be bothered with her, no way—not if they'd give her to me," said Haley. . . .

The conversation was interrupted by a busy hum in the audience; and the auctioneer, a short, bustling, important fellow, elbowed his way into the crowd. The old woman drew in her breath, and caught instinctively at her son.

"Keep close to yer mammy, Albert—close—dey'll put us up togeder," she said.

"Oh, mammy, I'm fear'd they won't," said the boy.

"Dey must, child; I can't live, no ways, if they don't," said the old creature, vehemently.

The stentorian tones of the auctioneer, calling out to clear the way, now announced that the sale was about to commence. A place was cleared, and the bidding began. . . .

"Come, now, young un," said the auctioneer, giving the boy a touch with his hammer, "be up and show your springs, now."

"Put us up togedder—togedder—do please, Mas'r," said the old woman, holding fast to her boy.

"Be off," said the man, gruffly, pushing her away; "you come last. Now, darkey, spring;" and, with the word, he pushed the boy toward the block, while a deep, heavy groan rose behind him. The boy paused and looked back; but there was no time to stay, and, dashing the tears from his large, bright eyes, he was up in a moment.

His fine figure, alert limbs, and bright face, raised an instant competition, and half a dozen bids simultaneously met the ear of the auctioneer. Anxious, half-frightened, he looked from side to side, as he heard the clatter of contending bids—now here, now there—till the hammer fell. Haley had got him. He was pushed from the block towards his new master, but stopped one moment and looked back, when his poor old mother, trembling in every limb, held out her shaking hands toward him.

"Buy me too, Mas'r; for de dear Lord's sake!—buy me—I shall die if you don't!"

"You'll die if I do, that's the kink of it," said Haley,—"no!" And he turned on his heel. . . .

The poor victims of the sale, who had been brought up in one place together for years, gathered round the despairing old mother, whose agony was pitiful to see.

"Couldn't dey leave me one? Mas'r allers said I should have one,—he did," she repeated over and over in heart-broken tones.

"Trust in the Lord, Aunt Hagar," said the oldest of the men, sorrowfully.

"What good will it do?" said she, sobbing passionately.

An illustration from Uncle Tom's Cabin *movingly depicts an auction sale. The buying and selling of slaves aroused widespread anger in the North. In 1865 President Abraham Lincoln said, "Whenever I hear anyone arguing for slavery, I feel a strong impulse to see it tried on him personally."*

AUTHOR

Harriet Beecher Stowe (1811–1896) was the wife and the daughter of ministers. She decided to write *Uncle Tom's Cabin* after Congress passed the Fugitive Slave Act in 1850. The act forced citizens to help catch runaway slaves. Stowe hoped her novel would awaken people to the evils of slavery.

RESPONSE

In nineteenth-century America, only the Bible outsold *Uncle Tom's Cabin.* More than 300,000 copies of the novel were snatched up within the first year of its publication. In ten years, more than two million copies had been sold. The novel forced many northerners to recognize the brutality of slavery. Many southerners hated the book, saying it was northern propaganda that distorted life on southern plantations. They accused Stowe of attempting to destroy national unity.

President Abraham Lincoln first met Mrs. Stowe during the Civil War in 1863. He said, "So you're the little woman who wrote the book that made this great war!"

THE EMANCIPATION PROCLAMATION

(SEPTEMBER 22, 1862)

ABRAHAM LINCOLN

Before signing the Emancipation Proclamation, President Lincoln said, "I never, in my life, felt more certain that I was doing right than I do in signing this paper."

On July 22, 1862, President Abraham Lincoln read to his cabinet a draft of an emancipation proclamation. Secretary of State William Seward suggested that Lincoln wait until the North had won a military victory in the Civil War. The northern triumph at the Battle of Antietam on September 17, 1863, provided Lincoln with his chance. Several days later he made public the Emancipation Proclamation. It directed that after January 1, 1863, all slaves in the states rebelling against the Union "shall be then, thenceforward, and forever free."

The Emancipation Proclamation signaled the beginning of the end of slavery in the United States and opened the door to full citizenship for African Americans.

One month before he issued the proclamation, President Lincoln wrote in a letter, "My paramount object in this struggle is to save the Union and is not either to save or to destroy slavery. If I could save the Union without freeing any slave, I would do it; and if I could do it by freeing all the slaves, I would do it; and if I could save it by freeing some and leaving others alone, I would also do that."

Whereas on the 22nd day of September, A.D. 1862, a proclamation was issued by the President of the United States, containing, among other things, the following, to wit:

That on the lst day of January, A.D. 1863, all persons held as slaves within any State or designated part of a State the people whereof shall then be in rebellion against the United States shall be then, thenceforward, and forever free; and the executive government of the United States, including the military and naval authority thereof, will recognize and maintain the freedom of such persons and will do no act or acts to repress such persons, or any of them, in any efforts they may make for their actual freedom.

That the executive will on the lst day of January aforesaid, by proclamation, designate the States and parts of States, if any, in which the people thereof, respectively, shall then be in rebellion against the United States; and the fact that any State or the people thereof shall on that day be in good faith represented in the Congress of the United States by members chosen thereto at elections wherein a majority of the qualified voters of such States shall have participated shall, in the absence of strong countervailing testimony, be deemed conclusive evidence that such State and the people thereof are not then in rebellion against the United States.

Now, therefore, I, Abraham Lincoln, President of the United States, by virtue of the power in me vested as Commander-in-Chief of the Army and Navy of the United States in time of actual armed rebellion against the authority and government of the United States, and as a fit and necessary war measure for suppressing said rebellion, do, on this lst day of January, A.D. 1863, and in accordance with my purpose so to do, publicly proclaimed for the full period of one hundred days from the first day above mentioned, order and designate as the States and parts of States wherein the people thereof, respectively, are this day in rebellion against the United States the following, to wit:

Arkansas, Texas, Louisiana (except the parishes of St. Bernard, Plaquemines, Jefferson, St. John, St. Charles, St. James, Ascension, Assumption, Terrebonne, Lafourche, St. Mary, St. Martin, and Orleans, including the city of New

Frederick Douglass, one of the most important African-American leaders in the nineteenth century, said, "I took the proclamation for a little more than it purported and saw in its spirit a life and power far beyond its letter."

Word of the proclamation spread quickly to southern slaves. They knew that their freedom was at hand. When they saw the northern armies coming, many simply stole away to the Union side or refused to work for their masters. By the end of the war, one Union soldier in eight was African American.

Orleans), Mississippi, Alabama, Florida, Georgia, South Carolina, North Carolina, and Virginia (except the forty-eight counties designated as West Virginia, and also the counties of Berkeley, Accomac, Northampton, Elizabeth City, York, Princess Anne, and Norfolk, including the cities of Norfolk and Portsmouth), and which excepted parts are for the present left precisely as if this proclamation were not issued.

And by virtue of the power and for the purpose aforesaid, I do order and declare that all persons held as slaves within said designated States and parts of States are, and henceforth shall be, free; and that the Executive Government of the United States, including the military and naval authorities thereof, will recognize and maintain the freedom of said persons.

And I hereby enjoin upon the people so declared to be free to abstain from all violence, unless in necessary self-defense; and I recommend to them that, in all causes when allowed, they labor faithfully for reasonable wages.

And I further declare and make known that such persons of suitable condition will be received into the armed service of the United States to garrison forts, positions, stations, and other places, and to man vessels of all sorts in said service.

And upon this act, sincerely believed to be an act of justice, warranted by the Constitution upon military necessity, I invoke the considerate judgment of mankind and the gracious favor of Almighty God.

In this illustration, a Union soldier reads the Emancipation Proclamation by torchlight to newly freed slaves.

This illustration shows Lincoln reading the Emancipation Proclamation to members of his cabinet.

AUTHOR

Abraham Lincoln (1809–1865) was the sixteenth president of the United States. He won the Republican nomination and then the presidential election in 1860, mainly because he was considered a moderate on the slavery issue. During the first year of the war, Lincoln hesitated to end slavery because he sensed that most northern whites did not support emancipation. He also worried that such a move might cost him the support of the states lying between the North and the Deep South like Kentucky and Missouri. These border states had not seceded with the states of the Deep South, but Lincoln was not sure that they would remain in the Union. But, as the war continued, he realized that public opinion in the North was starting to change in favor of emancipation. More confident also of the border states' continued support, he issued the proclamation.

RESPONSE

The immediate effect of the proclamation was to increase racial tensions. In the North, members of Lincoln's Republican party tended to support the document, while the opposing Democratic party criticized it out of fear of the potential power of free blacks. Many Southerners attacked the proclamation, saying it would cause slaves to rebel. However, both free blacks and slaves saw the proclamation as a beacon of hope.

Many antislavery groups thought President Lincoln should have freed the slaves in all the states. It is estimated that of the nation's four million slaves, about 830,000 were not freed by the provisions of the proclamation. It did not apply to the four slave states loyal to the Union (Delaware, Kentucky, Maryland, and Missouri) and did not affect slaves in southern and western territory held by Union forces.

THE GETTYSBURG ADDRESS

(NOVEMBER 19, 1863)

ABRAHAM LINCOLN

Many writers have reported that Lincoln wrote the address on the back of an envelope while riding on the train to Gettysburg. This story is not true. He planned the speech in advance and drafted five different versions. The final copy, written for publication in 1864, differed a little from the speech he gave. This final version is the only copy Lincoln signed.

In November, a new national cemetery was dedicated at Gettysburg, Pennsylvania. The North had won a great Civil War victory there three months earlier. About 50,000 soldiers had been killed or wounded at the Battle of Gettysburg. The famous orator Edward Everett was the main speaker at the dedication. He spoke for nearly two hours. Then President Abraham Lincoln stood up. He spoke for about two minutes. His 10-sentence address contains just 269 words. In simple language Lincoln remembered those who had died in the battle and reminded Northerners why they were fighting the war.

The Gettysburg Address is one of the most moving tributes ever made to those who died in war and to the ideals that led them to sacrifice their lives.

Lincoln was invited to speak at Gettysburg only a few weeks before the ceremony. Because everyone expected great things from the main speaker, Edward Everett, Lincoln was asked merely to make "a few appropriate remarks." The audience gathered for the ceremony included ordinary citizens as well as famous figures.

Four score and seven years ago our fathers brought forth on this continent, a new nation, conceived in liberty, and dedicated to the proposition that all men are created equal.

Now we are engaged in a great civil war, testing whether that nation or any nation so conceived and so dedicated, can long endure. We are met on a great battle-field of that war. We have come to dedicate a portion of that field, as a final resting place for those who here gave their lives that that nation might live. It is altogether fitting and proper that we should do this.

But, in a larger sense, we can not dedicate—we can not consecrate—we can not hallow—this ground. The brave men, living and dead, who struggled here, have consecrated it, far above our poor power to add or detract. The world will little note, nor long remember what we say here, but it can never forget what they did here. It is for us the living, rather, to be dedicated here to the unfinished work which they who fought here have thus far so nobly advanced. It is rather for us to be here dedicated to the great task remaining before us—that from these honored dead we take increased devotion to that cause for which they gave the last full measure of devotion—that we here highly resolve that these dead shall not have died in vain—that this nation, under God, shall have a new birth of freedom—and that government of the people, by the people, for the people, shall not perish from the earth.

This is a photograph of Civil War private Francis E. Brownell, 11th New York Infantry. One Union officer said about the Battle of Gettysburg, "I tried to ride over the field but could not, for dead and wounded lay too thick to guide a horse through them."

AUTHOR

Lincoln proved to be a shrewd commander in chief of the Union armies and a master at resolving political disputes. These qualities helped him win reelection in 1864. Abraham Lincoln is judged by many as the greatest American president, freeing the slaves and guiding the North to victory in the Civil War.

RESPONSE

The audience responded to Lincoln's speech by clapping politely. Lincoln felt his "little speech" was "a flat failure." Southern newspapers attacked the address, and many northern papers praised it. *Harpers Weekly* magazine said that Lincoln spoke "from the heart to the heart."

Lincoln held his second version as he spoke, but he made some changes during the address. One was to add the phrase "under God" to the last sentence.

THE FOURTEENTH AMENDMENT

(JULY 9, 1868)

The Fourteenth Amendment did not specifically prohibit segregation. In addition, a state might choose to prevent African Americans from voting, but there was a penalty: the state's representation in Congress would be reduced.

After the Civil War the Republican majority in Congress pushed through the Fourteenth Amendment. The amendment defined American citizenship to include all former slaves. It also declared that the states could not unlawfully deny any citizens their rights and privileges. The amendment is the first national document that granted major rights to the newly freed slaves.

Frederick Douglass was a crusader in the fight to end slavery and was recognized as one of America's first great black speakers. During the Civil War he served as an adviser to Abraham Lincoln, and later fought for the adoption of the Fourteenth Amendment. He realized that the struggle was not over when slavery ended and said, "Slavery is not abolished until the black man has the ballot."

Section 1. All persons born or naturalized in the United States, and subject to the jurisdiction thereof, are citizens of the United States and of the State wherein they reside. No State shall make or enforce any law which shall abridge the privileges or immunities of citizens of the United States; nor shall any State deprive any person of life, liberty, or property, without due process of law; nor deny to any person within its jurisdiction the equal protection of the laws.

Section 2. Representatives shall be apportioned among the several States according to their respective numbers, counting the whole number of persons in each State, excluding Indians not taxed. But when the right to vote at any election for the choice of electors for President and Vice President of the United States, Representatives in Congress, the Executive and Judicial officers of a State, or the members of the Legislature thereof, is denied to any of the male inhabitants of such State, being twenty-one years of age, and citizens of the United States, or in any way abridged, except for participating in rebellion, or other crime, the basis of representation therein shall be reduced in the proportion which the number of such male citizens shall bear to the whole number of male citizens twenty-one years of age in such State.

Section 3. No person shall be a Senator or Representative in Congress, or elector of President and Vice President, or hold any office, civil or military, under the United States, or under any State, who, having previously taken an oath, as a member of Congress, or as an officer of the United States, or as a member of any State legislature, or as an executive or judicial officer of any State, to support the Constitution of the United States, shall have engaged in insurrection or rebellion against the same, or given aid or comfort to the enemies thereof. But Congress may by a vote of two-thirds of each House, remove such disability.

Section 4. The validity of the public debt of the United States, authorized by law, including debts incurred for payment of pensions and bounties for services in suppressing insurrection or rebellion, shall not be questioned. But neither the United States nor any State shall assume or pay any debt or obligation incurred in aid of insurrection or rebellion against

President Johnson believed it was up to the states, and not the federal government, to make sure that the rights of African Americans were protected.

After the Civil War, many former slaves found themselves homeless and few had the skills necessary to build an independent life. The U.S. War Department established the Freedmen's Bureau in 1865 for the purpose of providing medical, educational, and financial assistance for the millions of impoverished southern African Americans.

The amendment also increased the power of the national government, while decreasing the power of the states. Now the federal government had the responsibility for guaranteeing all Americans their equal rights under the law.

the United States, or any claim for the loss or emancipation of any slave; but all such debts, obligations, and claims shall be held illegal and void.

Section 5. The Congress shall have the power to enforce, by appropriate legislation, the provisions of this article.

This photo shows Company E, 4th U.S. Colored Infantry, at Fort Lincoln, Washington, D.C. After the war, Congress passed the Fourteenth Amendment, making African Americans citizens and guaranteeing all citizens "the equal protection of the laws."

RESPONSE

By February 1867 nearly every southern and border state had rejected the Fourteenth Amendment. Republican radicals in Congress decided to pressure these states to support the amendment by making their readmission to the Union (after they had seceded and waged the Civil War) depend on their ratifying it. This strategy eventually worked, and seven southern states passed it in 1868. Enough states had now passed the amendment to make it the law of the land.

President Andrew Johnson (1808–1875) opposed the amendment. He made it the main issue of the 1866 congressional elections. But most Northerners had come to believe that African Americans should have the rights of citizens. Therefore, voters elected a large majority of Republicans who supported the amendment, which Congress passed in June 1866.

In July 1867, President Johnson asked Frederick Douglass to take charge of the Freedmen's Bureau. This was the first major government post offered to an African American. Douglass considered the request but then refused the position. He did not want to help Johnson, a man whose policies and beliefs he hated.

THE FIFTEENTH AMENDMENT

(FEBRUARY 3, 1870)

This illustration entitled The First Vote *appeared in the popular magazine* Harpers Weekly *in 1867. The men standing in line to vote represent the various professions of African Americans: a worker with his tools, a well-dressed middle-class man, and a Union soldier.*

By passing the Fifteenth Amendment, Republicans in Congress hoped to fulfill their promise of equality to African Americans in the aftermath of the Civil War. The amendment gave African-American males the vote.

Although the amendment opened the way for equality, the struggle continued for more than one hundred years. African Americans fought against continued oppression, forming organizations such as the National Association for the Advancement of Colored People (NAACP) in 1909. During the following century, leaders such as W. E. B. Du Bois, A. Philip Randolph, and Martin Luther King, Jr., led the struggle for equality. Their work resulted in the Voting Rights Act of 1965. The act ensured that African Americans and those of other ethnicities could freely exercise their right to vote.

Section 1. The right of citizens of the United States to vote shall not be denied or abridged by the United States or any State on account of race, color, or previous condition of servitude.

Section 2. The Congress shall have power to enforce this article by appropriate legislation.

The amendment said nothing about the right of African-American women to vote. This was not surprising—because no women had the right to vote until 1920.

RESPONSE

Most southern states had to pass the amendment because of pressure from the national government, and the amendment became law in February 1870. African Americans in the South began voting soon afterward. During the 1880s, they elected African Americans to offices throughout the South. However, in the 1890s, southern states began adding literacy tests and using other tactics that ended nearly all African-American voting in the South. Southern African Americans only began to vote again when the modern civil rights movement successfully began to challenge these tactics in the 1960s.

An illustration by the famous artists Currier and Ives features the first African-American senators and representatives in the 41st and 42nd Congress. All were elected from southern states. Senator Hiram Revels (left) was elected in 1870 to the seat that had been occupied by Jefferson Davis (the president of the Confederacy) when the South left the Union before the Civil War.

I Will Fight No More Forever

(OCTOBER 5, 1877)

Chief Joseph

This photograph is of Nez Percé chief Joseph. He once said, "We only ask an even chance to live as other men live. We ask to be recognized as men. We ask that the same law shall work alike on all men."

Before the government tried to force them onto a reservation, the Nez Percé were a peaceful tribe. They bred livestock, and their many horses and cattle grazed in the rich meadows on their lands.

In 1877 white settlers in Oregon wanted to take the lands of the Nez Percé Indians. The government responded to the settlers' land hunger by ordering the Nez Percé to remove themselves to a small reservation in Idaho. The Nez Percé refused, and war broke out between the tribe and the U.S. Army. After defeating the army in their first encounter, the Nez Percé realized that they would soon be hunted down. Therefore, they decided to flee to Canada. The trek was 1,300 miles. U.S. troops pursued the band of almost 600 Indians every step of the way, but the Nez Percé managed to evade them for nearly 75 days. Then, close to the Canadian border, the Nez Percé were trapped. His band surrounded, Chief Joseph was forced to surrender to the army.

Chief Joseph's speech is one of the most famous Native American documents. Probably no other Native American voice so powerfully describes the tragedy of Indian displacement and defeat. Chief Joseph's surrender in 1877 nearly marked the end of the Indian wars. No other big battle occurred until the last, the Battle of Wounded Knee, in 1890.

Tell General Howard I know his heart. What he told me before I have in my heart. I am tired of fighting. Our chiefs are killed. Looking Glass is dead. Too-hul-hul-sote is dead. The old men are all dead. It is the young men who say yes or no. He who led on the young men is dead. It is cold and we have no blankets. The little children are freezing to death. My people, some of them, have run away to the hills, and have no blankets, no food; no one knows where they are—perhaps freezing to death. I want to have time to look for my children and see how many of them I can find. Maybe I shall find them among the dead. Hear me, my chiefs. I am tired; my heart is sick and sad. From where the sun now stands I will fight no more forever.

Looking Glass was a Nez Percé warrior. He advised Chief Joseph against trying to make the dangerous escape attempt from Montana to Canada. A U.S. Army soldier shot and killed Looking Glass.

Chief Joseph's doctor attributed the warrior's death to a "broken heart."

In his speech Chief Joseph spoke of the death of "He who led on the young men." This was Ollokot, his younger brother.

AUTHOR

Chief Joseph (c. 1840–1904) was a great Native American warrior and leader. After his surrender, the federal government sent him and the surviving members of his tribe to the Indian Territory in present-day Oklahoma. There, most of the trek's survivors died of disease and starvation. Around 1885 Chief Joseph was moved to the Colville Indian Reservation in Washington, where he died in 1904.

RESPONSE

Many white Americans were moved by the bravery of the Nez Percé during their retreat. Even the commanding officers to whom Chief Joseph surrendered felt sympathetic to him. Many local whites, however, were happy to possess the Indians' lands.

STATEMENT ON THE CAUSES OF WOUNDED KNEE

(1890)

RED CLOUD

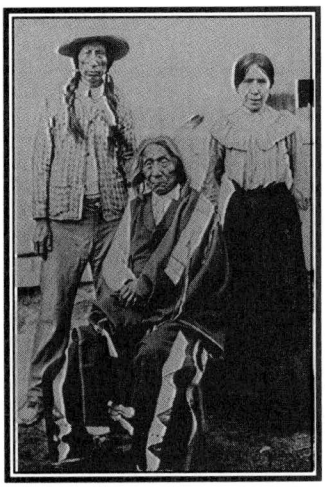

Chief Red Cloud poses with his son and granddaughter. At the time of this photograph, Red Cloud was ninety years old.

In 1889 a religious cult, based on the teachings of a Nevada Paiute named Wovoka, had sprung up among the Sioux Indians. Wovoka claimed that on Judgment Day an Indian Messiah would restore the lands that the Indians had lost to white Americans, who would then disappear. Wovoka also performed the Ghost Dance to make Judgment Day come sooner. The spread of the Ghost Dance ceremony among the Sioux alarmed local whites. They saw it as a sign that the Sioux were going to rise up against them, and tensions increased between whites and the Indians.

Fearing that the whites might massacre them, some three hundred Sioux fled. On December 29, 1890, the U.S. Army surrounded the Sioux at Wounded Knee Creek in South Dakota. The Indians raised a surrender flag. But a shot fired by a warrior caused the troops to open fire. In minutes, about 146 warriors lay dying. In this document, the Sioux warrior and chief Red Cloud describes the events leading up to the massacre.

I will tell you the reason for the trouble. When we first made treaties with the Government, our old life and our old customs were about to end; the game on which we lived was disappearing; the whites were closing around us, and nothing remained for us but to adopt their ways,—the Government promised us all the means necessary to make our living out of the land, and to instruct us how to do it, and with abundant food to support us until we could take care of ourselves. We looked forward with hope to the time we could be as independent as the whites, and have a voice in the Government.

The army officers could have helped better than anyone else but we were not left to them. An Indian Department was made with a large number of agents and other officials drawing large salaries—then came the beginning of trouble; these men took care of themselves but not of us. It was very hard to deal with the government through them—they could make more for themselves by keeping us back than by helping us forward.

We did not get the means for working our lands; the few things they gave us did little good.

Our rations began to be reduced; they said we were lazy. That is false. How does any man of sense suppose that so great a number of people could get work at once unless they were at once supplied with the means to work and instructors enough to teach them?

Our ponies were taken away from us under the promise that they would be replaced by oxen and large horses; it was long before we saw any, and then we got very few. We tried with the means we had, but on one pretext or another, we were shifted from one place to another, or were told that such a transfer was coming. Great efforts were made to break up our customs, but nothing was done to introduce us to customs of the whites. Everything was done to break up the power of the real chiefs.

Those old men really wished their people to improve, but little men, so-called chiefs, were made to act as disturbers and agitators. Spotted Tail wanted the ways of the whites, but an assassin was found to remove him. This was charged to the Indians because an Indian did it, but who set on the Indian? I was abused and slandered, to weaken my influence for good. This was done by men paid by the government to teach us the

The Ghost Dance chant begins: "The whole world is coming. / A nation is coming, a nation is coming. / The Eagle has brought the message to the tribe."

ways of the whites. I have visited many other tribes and found that the same things were done amongst them; all was done to discourage us and nothing to encourage us. I saw men paid by the government to help us, all very busy making money for themselves, but doing nothing for us. . . .

The men who counted (census) told all around that we were feasting and wasting food. Where did he see it? How could we waste what we did not have? We felt we were mocked in our misery; we had no newspaper and no one to speak for us. Our rations were again reduced.

You who eat three times a day and see your children well and happy around you cannot understand what a starving Indian feels! We were faint with hunger and maddened by despair. We held our dying children and felt their little bodies tremble as their soul went out and left only a dead weight in our hands. They were not very heavy but we were faint and the dead weighed us down. There was no hope on earth. God seemed to have forgotten.

Some one had been talking of the Son of God and said He had come. The people did not know; they did not care; they snatched at hope; they screamed like crazy people to Him for mercy; they caught at the promise they heard He had made.

The white people were frightened and called for soldiers. We begged for life and the white men thought we wanted theirs; we heard the soldiers were coming. We did not fear. We hoped we could tell them our suffering and could get help. The white men told us the soldiers meant to kill us; we did not believe it but some were frightened and ran away to the Bad Lands. The soldiers came. They said: "don't be afraid—we come to make peace, not war." It was true; they bought us food. But the hunger-crazed who had taken fright at the soldiers' coming and went to the Bad Lands could not be induced to return to the horrors of reservation life. They were called Hostiles and the Government sent the army to force them back to their reservation prison.

Big Foot's Minniconjou band was photographed at the Ghost Dance on the Cheyenne River on August 9, 1890. Four months later, nearly all were killed. The U.S. Army surrounded the Sioux at Wounded Knee Creek and turned their guns on them.

After they killed the Sioux warriors, the soldiers shot the Indian women and children who were attempting to run away from the battlefield.

AUTHOR

Red Cloud (1822–1909) was a great Sioux chief and warrior. Throughout the 1860s, he led the Sioux in a fight to keep white settlers out of Sioux lands in present-day South Dakota, Montana, and Wyoming. This struggle has been called Red Cloud's War. At its end, the army was forced to give up three forts it had built in the region and the government promised not to construct any roads through Sioux lands.

RESPONSE

The army had responded to the fears of settlers and government officials, who were relieved and happy at being protected from the Sioux. Those Sioux who had not been at Wounded Knee were filled with sadness. The tribe's Ghost Dance rites and rituals ended. The Battle of Wounded Knee ended the military warfare between the western Indians and whites.

Black Elk, a survivor of Wounded Knee, later said, "A terrible blizzard raged for two days covering the bodies with Nature's great white blanket; some lay in piles of four or five; others in twos or threes or singly, where they fell until the storm subsided."

This photo shows bodies on the battleground at Wounded Knee. One Indian later recalled the battle: "I can see that something else died there in the bloody mud, and was buried in the blizzard. A people's dream died there."

Twenty Years at Hull-House

(1910)

Jane Addams

This photograph shows Jane Addams reading to her nephew, Stanley R. Linn. While at Hull-House, Addams discovered that slum children needed to be taught more than just reading and writing. She believed that this type of education "fails to give the child any clue to the life about him."

By the late 1890s increasing numbers of American reformers were focusing on helping the urban poor. The reformers organized community centers in slum areas, where many immigrants lived. The centers, or settlement houses, offered neighborhood people services and guidance. In 1889 Jane Addams and her college friend Ellen Starr founded Hull-House on Halsted Street, in one of Chicago's worst slums. Addams and the other settlement workers lived in Hull-House. It grew to have a nursery, a kindergarten, a gymnasium, and a playground, and offered activities such as music and art classes.

By 1900 about 100 settlement houses had been established across the country. Hull-House served as a model for many of them. Addams's work caused many Americans to support the need for social reform. Today, largely because of her efforts, community centers and settlement houses exist in cities across the United States. In 1910 she wrote about her experiences as a reformer in *Twenty Years at Hull-House*. The following passage is from Chapter 5, "First Days at Hull-House."

. . . The dozens of younger children who from the first came to Hull-House were organized into groups which were not quite classes and not quite clubs. The values of these groups consisted almost entirely in arousing a higher imagination and in giving the children the opportunity which they could not have in the crowded schools, for initiative and for independent social relationships. The public schools then contained little hand work of any sort, so that naturally any instruction which we provided for the children took the direction of this supplementary work. But it required a constant effort that the pressure of poverty itself should not defeat the educational aim. The Italian girls in the sewing classes would count that day lost when they could not carry home a garment, and the insistence that it should be neatly made seemed a super-refinement to those in dire need of clothing.

As these clubs have been continued during the twenty years they have developed classes in the many forms of handicraft which the newer education is so rapidly adapting for the delight of children; but they still keep their essentially social character and still minister to that large number of children who leave school the very week they are fourteen years old, only too eager to close the schoolroom door forever on a tiresome task that is at last well over. It seems to us important that these children shall find themselves permanently attached to a House that offers them evening clubs and classes with their old companions, that merges as easily as possible the school life into the working life and does what it can to find places for the bewildered young things looking for work. A large proportion of the delinquent boys brought into the juvenile court in Chicago are the oldest sons in large families whose wages are needed at home. The grades from which many of them leave school, as the records show, are piteously far from the seventh and eighth where the very first instruction in manual training [course of training to develop skill in using the hands and to teach practical arts such as woodworking and metalworking] is given, nor have they been caught by any other abiding interest. . . .

In those early days we were often asked why we had come to live on Halsted Street when we could afford to live somewhere else. I remember one man who used to shake his head

Hull-House stood on five-mile-long Halsted Street, which teemed with Irish, German, Russian, Italian, and Polish immigrants.

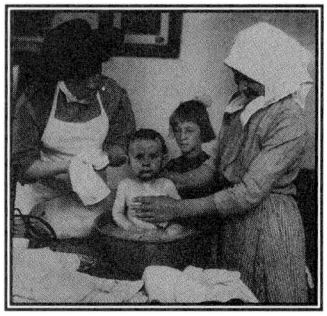

At Hull-House visiting nurses taught mothers how to better care for their children. In this photograph, a nurse shows a mother how to properly bathe her baby.

Jane Addams was only twenty-nine when she and Ellen Starr established Hull-House in an old mansion. Addams never moved from Hull-House, which expanded to include 13 buildings.

and say it was "the strangest thing he had met in his experience," but who was finally convinced that it was "not strange but natural." In time it came to seem natural to all of us that the Settlement should be there. It is natural to feed the hungry and care for the sick, it is certainly natural to give pleasure to the young, comfort to the aged, and to minister to the deep-seated craving for social intercourse that all men feel. Whoever does it is rewarded by something which, if not gratitude, is at least spontaneous and vital and lacks that irksome sense of obligation with which a substantial benefit is too often acknowledged.

In addition to the neighbors who responded to the receptions and classes, we found those who were too battered and oppressed to care for them. To these, however, was left that susceptibility to the bare offices [acts] of humanity which raises such offices into a bond of fellowship.

From the first it seemed understood that we were ready to perform the humblest neighborhood services. We were asked to wash the newborn babies, and to prepare the dead for burial, to nurse the sick, and to "mind the children." . . .

We were also early impressed with the curious isolation of many of the immigrants; an Italian woman once expressed her pleasure in the red roses that she saw at one of our receptions in surprise that they had been "brought so fresh all the way from Italy." She would not believe for an instant that they had been grown in America. She said that she had lived in Chicago for six years and had never seen any roses, whereas in Italy she had seen them every summer in great profusion. During all that time, of course, the woman had lived within ten blocks of a florist's window; she had not been more than a five-cent car ride away from the public parks; but she had never dreamed of faring forth for herself, and no one had taken her. Her conception of America had been the untidy street in which she lived and had made her long struggle to adapt herself to American ways.

But in spite of some untoward experiences, we were constantly impressed with the uniform kindness and courtesy we received. Perhaps these first days laid the simple human foundations which are certainly essential for continuous living among the poor: first, genuine preference for residence in an industrial quarter to any other part of the city, because it is interesting and makes the human appeal; and second, the conviction . . . that the things which make men alike are finer and better than the things that keep them apart, and that these basic likenesses, if they are properly accentuated, easily transcend the less essential differences of race, language, creed, and tradition.

Perhaps even in those first days we made a beginning toward that object which was afterward stated in our charter: "To provide a center for a higher civic and social life; to institute and maintain educational and philanthropic enterprises, and to investigate and improve the conditions in the industrial districts of Chicago."

The immigrant families that Hull-House and other settlement houses served often lived in cities in overcrowded, run-down buildings called tenements. The famous photographer Jacob Riis took this photograph of an Italian immigrant family of seven living in a one-room tenement apartment around 1890.

AUTHOR

Born into a prosperous Illinois family, Jane Addams (1860–1935) became interested in reform work while traveling in Europe. The example of English reformers who voluntarily lived in London slums moved her to found Hull-House. Although she remained committed to Hull-House, Addams soon realized that real reform could come about only through legislation. So she entered politics. She and her supporters helped to end child labor, limit the hours of working women, and set up the juvenile court system. During the last years of her life, she organized women around the world for peace. In 1931 she became the first American woman to win the Nobel Peace Prize.

Most settlement house workers were young women. Some had just graduated from college. One British visitor described the workers at Hull-House as "strong-minded and energetic women, bustling about their various enterprises." Another visitor said Jane Addams was "the only saint the United States has produced."

RESPONSE

Jane Addams was the most admired woman of her time. She used her account of Hull-House to publicize the reform movement and her own work. Many Americans approved of some, if not all, of the practical reforms she made or desired. But a few critics argued that settlement houses were bandages that did not really cure the troubles of the poor.

THE SIXTEENTH AMENDMENT

(FEBRUARY 25, 1913)

In the 1860s, the huge costs of the Civil War pushed Congress to pass the first federal income tax. This Internal Revenue Service Act placed a 3-percent tax on all incomes above $800. A new bureau, the Internal Revenue Bureau, directed the collection of taxes. Congress repealed that tax in 1872.

The Constitution did not allow the federal government to collect taxes from citizens. In 1909 reformers in Congress tried to pass a bill that included a federal income tax. Congressional conservatives hit upon a plan to permanently kill the idea. Sure that it would never be ratified, in July 1909 they proposed a constitutional amendment imposing such a tax. Imagine their surprise when the states easily passed the amendment! Many historians have called this amendment the most significant reform of the twentieth century. It provided the federal government with the money to pay for new social programs to help the poor and the elderly. Without the amendment, the nation also would not have had the financial resources to conduct wars such as World War II.

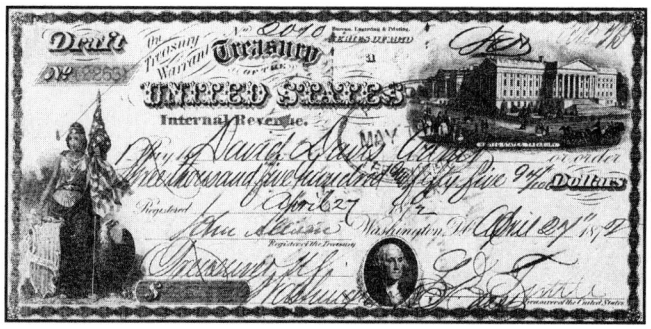

After Congress imposed the first income tax in 1861, President Lincoln dutifully paid; but, under the terms of the 1872 Internal Services Act, presidents did not have to pay. Seven years after Lincoln was assassinated, the government sent this refund to his family for $3,555.94.

The Congress shall have power to lay and collect taxes on incomes, from whatever source derived, without apportionment among the several States, and without regard to any census or enumeration.

RESPONSE

The idea of a personal income tax was popular because many believed that the rich would bear most of the tax burden. Only conservative Republicans and the wealthy did not support the amendment.

U. S. TREASURY DEPARTMENT
BUREAU OF INTERNAL REVENUE
INTELLIGENCE UNIT

WANTED FOR VIOLATION OF

Federal Income Tax Law

PLEASE CLASSIFY AND FILE WITH FINGERPRINT RECORDS

FLEGENHEIMER

RIGHT HAND

LEFT HAND

ARTHUR FLEGENHEIMER, alias DUTCH SCHULTZ
ARTHUR SCHULTZ, GEORGE SCHULTZ, JOSEPH HARMON AND CHARLES HARMON.
DESCRIPTION—Age 34 years; height 5 feet, 7 inches; weight 165 pounds; medium build; brown hair; gray eyes; fair complexion. B-50149.

HENRY MARGOLIS, alias HENRY STEVENS
DESCRIPTION—Age 37 years; height 5 feet, 7 inches; weight 180 pounds; stocky build; light chestnut brown hair; brown eyes; ruddy complexion. B-95758.

MARGOLIS

RIGHT HAND

LEFT HAND

Flegenheimer is under indictment jointly with Henry Margolis (alias Henry Stevens), Frank J. Ahearn and George Yarlasavetsky (alias George Yarlas, alias George Young).

Frank J. Ahearn is white, 5 feet 11 inches tall, about 34 years of age, blue eyes, brown hair and weighs 160 pounds.

George Yarlasavetsky is white, about 5 feet 8 inches tall, 32 years old, green eyes, brown hair, reddish moustache, weighs about 140 pounds and is an accountant by profession.

If located, arrest and hold as a fugitive from justice, and advise, by wire:
Hugh McQuillan, Special Agent in Charge, Intelligence Unit,
Room 1, Old Post Office Building, New York, N. Y.
Telephone: Courtlandt 7-1420.

This 1934 "Wanted" poster issued by the United States Treasury shows two men who were wanted by the government for violation of the federal income tax law.

During the 1930s the government started to use the Sixteenth Amendment to get gangsters off the streets and into jails. The government imprisoned gang leaders such as Chicago's Al Capone on charges that they evaded paying income tax on the huge amounts of money they made illegally.

THE FOURTEEN POINTS

(JANUARY 8, 1918)

WOODROW WILSON

President Wilson waves his hat to crowds in this photo taken during his tour of Europe after World War I. During the war American pilots dropped leaflets over Germany describing Wilson's Fourteen Points. The Americans hoped the German people would read these leaflets and be persuaded to end the war.

For three years President Woodrow Wilson kept the United States out of World War I. But in 1917 he reluctantly joined France, England, and their allies in the struggle against Germany. American intervention brought victory for the Allies and gave Wilson the opportunity to try to establish permanent peace among the world's nations. Early in 1918 he delivered a speech to Congress outlining a plan to make the world "fit and safe to live in." Wilson's peace plan, which had 14 separate items, became known as the Fourteen Points. The first five points stated general principles for positive international conduct such as free trade between nations. Eight other points involved setting new boundaries in Europe after the war and creating several new countries. The fourteenth point called for a League of Nations to put into action these principles and to resolve future international disputes.

...We entered this war because violations of right had occurred which touched us to the quick and made the life of our own people impossible unless they were corrected and the world secured once for all against their recurrence. What we demand in this war, therefore, is nothing peculiar to ourselves. It is that the world be made fit and safe to live in; and particularly that it be made safe for every peace-loving nation which, like our own, wishes to live its own life, determine its own institutions, be assured of justice and fair dealing by the other peoples of the world as against force and selfish aggression. All the peoples of the world are in effect partners in this interest, and for our own part we see very clearly that unless justice be done to others it will not be done to us. The program of the world's peace, therefore, is our program; and that program, the only possible program as we see it, is this:

I. Open covenants of peace, openly arrived at, after which there shall be no private international understandings of any kind but diplomacy shall proceed always frankly and in the public view.

II. Absolute freedom of navigation upon the seas, outside territorial waters, alike in peace and in war, except as the seas

In this photo the Allied leaders meet with Woodrow Wilson at the Paris Peace Conference in 1919. David Lloyd George of Great Britain, Vittorio Orlando of Italy, and Georges Clemenceau of France all favored a more traditional settlement for peace. Wilson worked tirelessly for a peace outlined in his Fourteen Points.

Woodrow Wilson began his career as a university professor. While teaching at Bryn Mawr College, Wesleyan University, and Princeton University, he wrote nine books and more than 35 articles on politics and history. After serving as president of Princeton from 1902 to 1910, he was elected governor of New Jersey.

may be closed in whole or in part by international action for the enforcement of international covenants.

III. The removal, so far as possible, of all economic barriers and the establishment of an equality of trade conditions among all the nations consenting to the peace and associating themselves for its maintenance.

IV. Adequate guarantees given and taken that national armaments will be reduced to the lowest point consistent with domestic safety.

V. A free, open-minded, and absolutely impartial adjustment of all colonial claims, based upon a strict observance of the principle that in determining all such questions of sovereignty the interests of the populations concerned must have equal weight with the equitable claims of the government whose title is to be determined.

VI. The evacuation of all Russian territory and such a settlement of all questions affecting Russia as will secure the best and freest cooperation of the other nations of the world in obtaining for her an unhampered and unembarrassed opportunity for the independent determination of her own political development and national policy and assure her of a sincere welcome into the society of free nations under institutions of her own choosing; and, more than a welcome, assistance also of every kind that she may need and may herself desire. The treatment accorded Russia by her sister nations in the months to come will be the acid test of their good will, of their comprehension of her needs as distinguished from their own interests, and of their intelligent and unselfish sympathy.

VII. Belgium, the whole world will agree, must be evacuated and restored, without any attempt to limit the sovereignty which she enjoys in common with all other free nations. No other single act will serve as this will serve to restore confidence among the nations in the laws which they have themselves set and determined for the government of their relations with one another. Without this healing act the whole structure and validity of international law is forever impaired.

VIII. All French territory should be freed and the invaded portions restored, and the wrong done to France by Prussia in 1871 in the matter of Alsace-Lorraine, which has unsettled the peace of the world for nearly fifty years, should be righted, in order that peace may once more be made secure in the interest of all.

IX. A readjustment of the frontiers of Italy should be effected along clearly recognizable lines of nationality.

X. The peoples of Austria-Hungary, whose place among the nations we wish to see safeguarded and assured, should be accorded the freest opportunity of autonomous development.

XI. Rumania, Serbia, and Montenegro should be evacuated; occupied territories restored; Serbia accorded free and secure access to the sea; and the relations of the several Balkan states to one another determined by friendly counsel along historically established lines of allegiance and nationality; and international guarantees of the political and economic independence and territorial integrity of the several Balkan states should be entered into.

XII. The Turkish portions of the present Ottoman Empire should be assured a secure sovereignty, but the other nationalities which are now under the Turkish rule should be assured an undoubted security of life and an absolutely unmolested opportunity of autonomous development, and the Dardanelles should be permanently opened as a free passage to the ships and commerce of all nations under international guarantees.

XIII. An independent Polish state should be erected which should include the territories inhabited by indisputably Polish populations, which should be assured a free and secure access to the sea, and whose political and economic independence and territorial integrity should be guaranteed by international covenant.

Woodrow Wilson's unsuccessful attempt to keep America out of the war was personally exhausting. He lost sleep and looked pale and tired. When someone asked which side he hoped would win the war, Wilson said, "Neither."

XIV. A general association of nations must be formed under specific covenants for the purpose of affording mutual guarantees of political independence and territorial integrity to great and small states alike. . . .

We have spoken now, surely, in terms too concrete to admit of any further doubt or question. An evident principle runs through the whole program I have outlined. It is the principle of justice to all peoples and nationalities, and their right to live on equal terms of liberty and safety with one another, whether they be strong or weak. Unless this principle be made its foundation no part of the structure of international justice can stand. The people of the United States could act upon no other principle; and to the vindication of this principle they are ready to devote their lives, their honor, and everything that they possess. The moral climax of this the culminating and final war for human liberty has come, and they are ready to put their own strength, their own highest purpose, their own integrity and devotion to the test.

President Woodrow Wilson was cheered as a hero during his 1919 visit to Dover, England. But at home the peace treaty that he had helped draw up was in trouble in Congress. On Wilson's return, he made as many as four speeches a day to persuade Americans to support the treaty, which established the League of Nations. He felt sure the League was necessary to prevent another world war. But he failed in his attempt, and the United States never joined the League of Nations.

AUTHOR

Woodrow Wilson (1856–1924) was the twenty-eighth president of the United States. Before entering politics, he served as president of Princeton University in New Jersey. In 1910 he became the Democratic governor of New Jersey. Two years later he was elected president on the Democratic ticket. At the outbreak of World War I, Wilson, who hated war, tried desperately to preserve American neutrality. But when Germany continued to attack United States ships with their submarines, he asked Congress to declare war. In October 1919 Wilson suffered a stroke at the end of a nationwide speaking tour to defend the peace treaty and the League of Nations. Although he completed his term, Wilson never fully recovered.

RESPONSE

The 1919 Treaty of Versailles, which ended World War I, proposed what Wilson dreamed of—an international peacekeeping organization called the League of Nations. But some Americans disagreed with the idea. Henry Cabot Lodge, the powerful Republican senator from Massachusetts, led other senators in demanding changes in the treaty. But the president refused to compromise with Lodge. Wilson felt any changes would weaken the League. He failed to drum up enough public support for the treaty, and it was defeated in Congress on March 19, 1920. The United States finally signed a separate peace with Germany in July 1921.

Without the United States, the League of Nations was too weak to prevent World War II. But, as that war ended, Americans realized the necessity of a strong world peacekeeping organization to replace the League. When the United Nations met for the first time in London, England, on January 10, 1946, the United States was a full member.

Premier Clemenceau of France was not enthusiastic about Wilson's plan. "God gave us the Ten Commandments and we broke them," he said. "Wilson gave us the Fourteen Points. We shall see."

THE NINETEENTH AMENDMENT

(AUGUST 18, 1920)

The officers of the National American Woman Suffrage Association pose in this 1919 photo. After the passage of the Nineteenth Amendment, Carrie Chapman Catt said to supporters: "Ours has been a movement with a soul, ever leading on. Women came, served, and passed on, but others came to take their places."

Before the passage of the Nineteenth Amendment, American women had almost no legal, political, or social rights. They could not vote, own property, or gain custody of their children. Many women realized that the only way to gain these rights was through the power of the ballot. So from the late 1860s on, women organized and petitioned state legislatures and Congress to give them the vote. Their efforts met with intense opposition by both male and female antisuffragists. But this did not stop them. In 1916 suffragists picketed the White House, facing arrest and even jail. Congress finally gave in to the pressure and passed the Nineteenth Amendment in May 1919. On August 18, 1920, the "Susan B. Anthony Amendment," as it was later called, had been ratified by the necessary 36 states and became part of the Constitution. With the Nineteenth Amendment, women finally won a voice in their government.

In 1872 women could not vote. But the National American Woman Suffrage Association backed Victoria Woodhull, the first woman to run for president of the United States. In 1872 Woodhull was the candidate of a new party called the Equal Rights Party.

Section 1. The right of citizens of the United States to vote shall not be denied or abridged by the United States or by any State on account of sex.

Section 2. Congress shall have power to enforce this article by appropriate legislation.

By the 1890s, millions of American women supported the independent suffrage movement.

AUTHORS

Although they did not specifically write the proposed amendment, Susan B. Anthony (1820–1906) and Carrie Chapman Catt (1859–1947) were among the most influential leaders of the American women's suffrage movement. Born to a middle-class family in Massachusetts, Susan Anthony became a teacher. Through her speeches and writing, she also roused generations of American women to the awareness that suffrage was their right. In 1900 she stepped down from the presidency of the National American Woman Suffrage Association (NAWSA). Anthony chose Carrie Chapman Catt as her successor in that position. The Wisconsin-born Catt, who, like Anthony, was a teacher, rose quickly in the suffragist movement. An excellent strategist, Catt enlisted and directed volunteers, spoke everywhere, organized events, and used the media to promote womans suffrage. Over the next 20 years, she led the movement to victory.

After the Nineteenth Amendment became law, Catt said, "To get the word 'male' in effect out of the Constitution cost the women of the country fifty-two years of pauseless campaign. . . ."

RESPONSE

Many activists were satisfied with what they had won. These moderates joined the recently formed League of Women Voters, whose main goal was to educate women on the issues so that they could vote intelligently. More militant suffragists felt, however, that they had not yet achieved total equality with men. In 1923 they founded the National Women's Party, which began campaigning for a constitutional Equal Rights Amendment (ERA). Congress finally passed the amendment in 1972, but only 35 of the 38 states required for ratification subsequently approved it. So, by the end of 1982, the amendment died.

In February 1917 suffragists picketed outside the White House to persuade President Wilson to support the right of women to vote. The police arrested the pickets for "obstructing traffic," but later that year Wilson spoke out for the first time in support of woman suffrage.

THE IMMIGRATION ACT

(MAY 26, 1924)

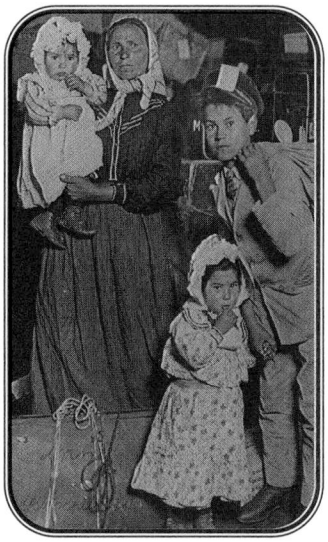

This photograph of an Italian immigrant family on Ellis Island was taken by Lewis Wickes Hine. His portraits of the immigrant life exposed the wretched housing and terrible working conditions that many immigrants were subjected to in their new homeland.

From its beginnings, the United States considered itself the land of immigrants. In the early twentieth century, a new wave of immigrants, mainly from southern and eastern Europe, flocked to this country. Many Americans, particularly members of the labor unions, became worried that the newcomers would take away their jobs. Congress responded to their pressure by passing the Immigration Act of 1924. The act limited immigration to 2 percent of each nationality present in the United States in the year 1890. At that time, only small numbers of eastern and southern European newcomers had entered.

The Immigration Act marked a turning point in the nation's history. For the first time, the government set broad restrictions on the number of newcomers. The act greatly reduced the number of legal immigrants while discriminating against immigrants from countries outside of northern Europe and against nonwhites. The following selection is from this act.

BY THE PRESIDENT OF
THE UNITED STATES OF AMERICA
A PROCLAMATION

Whereas it is provided in the act of Congress approved May 26, 1924, entitled "An act to limit the immigration of aliens into the United States, and for other purposes" that—

"The annual quota of any nationality shall be two per cent of the number of foreign-born individuals of such nationality resident in continental United States as determined by the United States census of 1890, but the minimum quota of any nationality shall be 100. . . ."

Now, therefore, I, Calvin Coolidge, President of the United States of America acting under and by virtue of power in me vested by the aforesaid act of Congress, do hereby proclaim and make known that on and after July 2, 1924, and throughout the fiscal year 1924–1925, the quota of each nationality provided in said Act shall be as follows:

Country or area of birth	*Quota 1924–1925*
Afghanistan	100
Albania	100
Andorra	100
Arabian peninsula	100
Armenia	124
Australia, including Papua, Tasmania, and all islands appertaining to Australia	121
Austria	785
Belgium	512
Bhutan	100
Bulgaria	100
Cameroon (proposed British mandate)	100
Cameroon (French mandate)	100
China	100
Czechoslovakia	3,073

This 1917 poster from the Cleveland Board of Education and the Cleveland Americanization Committee used six languages—English, Italian, Slovene, Polish, Hungarian, and Yiddish—to advertise free classes where immigrants could "learn the language of America" and "prepare for American Citizenship." Before the 1880s, most immigrants had come from northern Europe. The similarity of their customs, language, and religion to those of earlier Americans made it fairly easy for them to fit into society. Later, more and more of the newcomers came from southern and eastern Europe, and their differences seemed greater.

By the 1890s, Ellis Island, in New York City's harbor, became the major center for immigrants entering the United States.

"HELP!"
—Cargill in the Kansas City *Journal*

This cartoon pokes fun at the Unites States's "open arms policy." Europe, represented by the woman, holds a bundle of hungry and crying children, which are meant to represent Europe's "surplus populations." She asks America, here shown as an overwhelmed Uncle Sam, to "just hold these too Sam." Some criticisms were not so lighthearted. In an anti-immigrant petition from Philadelphia, citizens denounced the powers of Europe, claiming they were "disgorging their disgusting population into the very bosom of American society."

The 1924 restrictions on immigration did not apply to Mexico, Canada, or any other nation in North or South America.

Danzig, Free City of	228
Denmark	2,789
Egypt	100
Estonia	124
Ethiopia (Abyssinia)	100
Finland	170
France	3,954
Germany	51,227
Great Britain and Northern Ireland	34,007
Greece	100
Hungary	473
Iceland	100
India	100
Iraq (Mesopotamia)	100
Irish Free State	28,567
Italy, including Rhodes, Dodekanesia, and Castellorizzo	3,845
Japan	100
Latvia	142
Liberia	100
Liechtenstein	100
Lithuania	344
Luxemburg	100
Monaco	100
Morocco (French and Spanish Zones and Tangier)	100
Muscat (Oman)	100
Nauru (proposed British mandate)	100
Nepal	100
Netherlands	1,648
New Zealand (including appertaining islands)	100
Norway	6,453
New Guinea, and other Pacific Islands under proposed Australian mandate	100
Palestine (with Trans-Jordan, proposed British mandate)	100
Persia	100

Poland	5,982
Portugal	1,503
Ruanda and Urundi (Belgium mandate)	100
Rumania	603
Russia, European and Asiatic	2,248
Samoa, Western (proposed mandate of New Zealand)	100
San Marino	100
Siam	100
South Africa, Union of	100
South West Africa (proposed mandate of Union of South Africa)	100
Spain	131
Sweden	9,561
Switzerland	2,081
Syria and The Lebanon (French mandate)	100
Tanganyika (proposed British mandate)	100
Togoland (proposed British mandate)	100
Turkey	100
Yap and other Pacific islands (under Japanese mandate)	100
Yugoslavia	671

GENERAL NOTE—The immigration quotas assigned to the various countries and quota-areas should not be regarded as having any political significance whatever, or as involving recognition of new governments, or of new boundaries, or of transfers of territory except as the United States Government has already made such recognition in a formal and official manner. . . .

It took the Immigration Act of 1965 to end national quotas for immigration.

A photograph portrays immigrants arriving in New York Harbor from Hamburg, Germany, on the SS Patricia *on December 10, 1906. This boat carried 162 first-class passengers, 184 second-class passengers, and 2,100 steerage passengers. The steerage section of a ship had the worst accommodations and was occupied by poorer passengers. Because the fare to the United States was so expensive, most immigrants traveled in steerage.*

RESPONSE

The quota system immediately almost shut down immigration from eastern and southern Europe. Since most people who wanted to come to the United States were from those areas, the number of immigrants dropped dramatically.

A worker in California reads the news of Pearl Harbor. The attack shocked Americans. One sixteen-year-old witness who watched the injured come in recalled, "With the first sailor, so horribly burned, personal fear left me; it brought me the full tragedy of the day."

War Message to Congress

(DECEMBER 8, 1941)

Franklin Delano Roosevelt

On Sunday, December 7, the Japanese launched a surprise air attack on the United States naval base at Pearl Harbor in Hawaii. More than 2,300 Americans died in the early-morning bombing, which also destroyed most of the Pacific air force fleet. Americans were shocked, saddened, and outraged. The next day, President Roosevelt asked Congress to declare war on Japan. Later, the United States went to war with Japan's allies, Germany and Italy. Germany wanted to conquer Europe; Japan sought to control the Pacific area. Neither country was a democracy like the United States.

World War II ended in victory for the Allies. The United States and the United Soviet Socialist Republic (USSR) emerged as the two superpowers.

President Roosevelt wrote his war message almost entirely by himself. Fueled by his outrage about the attack on Pearl Harbor, he wrote swiftly. He had been advised to write a long description of Japanese behavior that led him to this point. Instead, the president decided on a brief message.

Yesterday, December 7, 1941—a day which will live in infamy—the United States of America was suddenly and deliberately attacked by naval and air forces of the empire of Japan.

The United States was at peace with that nation and, at the solicitation of Japan, was still in conversation with its government and its emperor looking toward the maintenance of peace in the Pacific.

Indeed, one hour after Japanese air squadrons had commenced bombing in the American Island of Oahu the Japanese Ambassador to the United States and his colleague delivered to our Secretary of State a formal reply to a recent American message. And, while this reply stated that it seemed useless to continue the existing diplomatic negotiations, it contained no threat or hint of war or of armed attack.

It will be recorded that the distance of Hawaii from Japan makes it obvious that the attack was deliberately planned many days or even weeks ago. During the intervening time the Japanese Government has deliberately sought to deceive the United States by false statements and expressions of hope for continued peace.

The attack yesterday on the Hawaiian Islands has caused severe damage to American naval and military forces. I regret to tell you that very many American lives have been lost. In addition American ships have been reported torpedoed on the high seas between San Francisco and Honolulu.

Yesterday the Japanese Government also launched an attack against Malaya.

Last night Japanese forces attacked Hong Kong.

Last night Japanese forces attacked Guam.

Last night Japanese forces attacked the Philippine Islands.

Last night the Japanese attacked Wake Island.

And this morning the Japanese attacked Midway Island.

Japan has therefore undertaken a surprise offensive extending throughout the Pacific area. The facts of yesterday and today speak for themselves. The people of the United States have already formed their opinions and well understand the implications to the very life and safety of our nation.

As Commander in Chief of the Army and the Navy, I have

Before the attack on Pearl Harbor, an American code expert had cracked the Japanese diplomatic code. American military experts now knew that the Japanese were up to something. But they expected them to target somewhere in Southeast Asia, perhaps in the Philippines. The experts dismissed the idea that Pearl Harbor would be attacked because it was too close to the United States mainland.

The most famous words in Roosevelt's war message were not in his original draft. That draft read, "Yesterday, December 7, 1941, a date which will live in world history. . ." Almost immediately, he scratched out this wording and substituted, "a date which will live in infamy."

directed that all measures be taken for our defense.

Always will our whole nation remember the character of the onslaught against us.

No matter how long it may take us to overcome this premeditated invasion, the American people in their righteous might will win through to absolute victory.

I believe that I interpret the will of the Congress and of the people when I assert that we will not only defend ourselves to the uttermost but will make it very certain that this form of treachery shall never again endanger us.

Hostilities exist. There is no blinking at the fact that our people, our territory and our interests are in grave danger.

With confidence in our armed forces, with the unbounding determination of our people, we will gain the inevitable triumph. So help us God.

I ask that Congress declare that since the unprovoked and dastardly attack by Japan on Sunday, Dec. 7, 1941, a state of war has existed between the United States and the Japanese Empire.

A day before the attack on Pearl Harbor, the president learned that the Japanese had rejected any attempt to resolve differences between America and Japan. Roosevelt then said, "This means war."

A dramatic photo shows the USS California *sinking after the surprise attack at Pearl Harbor on December 7, 1941. Months later, the sunken ship was refloated and repaired. The* California *went on to win seven battle stars in World War II.*

President Roosevelt signed the declaration of war against Japan just one day after the surprise attack on Pearl Harbor. Standing behind him are (from left to right) Senators Charles McNary, Alben Barkley, Carter Glass, Warren Austin, and Tom Connally.

By the morning of December 8, the White House was on the alert in case of a surprise attack. Before the president read his war message, the White House staff was being fitted for gas masks, blackout curtains were being measured to cover the windows, and extra police had surrounded the building.

Out of the war came a new technology of destruction—the atom bomb, which the United States secretly developed and then dropped on the Japanese cities of Hiroshima and Nagasaki in 1945 to force Japan to surrender.

AUTHOR

After the United States entered World War II, Franklin Roosevelt proved to be a skilled commander in chief. As it became increasingly clear that the Allies would defeat Germany and Japan, he prepared the nation to assume the leadership of the postwar world. Exhausted by his efforts overseeing the war, Roosevelt died of natural causes in April 1945. The only president to be elected four times, he was mourned by the entire nation.

RESPONSE

At 12:30 in the afternoon of December 8, Franklin Delano Roosevelt read his war message to Congress. The nation immediately united under the president's leadership. Congress voted almost unanimously to declare war against Japan. Three days later, Germany and Italy declared war against the United States. America had entered World War II.

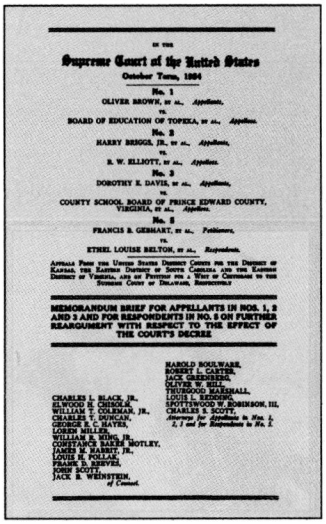

IN THE

Supreme Court of the United States

October Term, 1954

No. 1

OLIVER BROWN, ET AL., *Appellants*,

vs.

BOARD OF EDUCATION OF TOPEKA, ET AL., *Appellees*.

No. 2

HARRY BRIGGS, JR., ET AL., *Appellants*,

vs.

R. W. ELLIOTT, ET AL., *Appellees*.

No. 3

DOROTHY E. DAVIS, ET AL., *Appellants*,

vs.

COUNTY SCHOOL BOARD OF PRINCE EDWARD COUNTY, VIRGINIA, ET AL., *Appellees*.

No. 5

FRANCIS B. GEBHART, ET AL., *Petitioners*,

vs.

ETHEL LOUISE BELTON, ET AL., *Respondents*.

APPEALS FROM THE UNITED STATES DISTRICT COURTS FOR THE DISTRICT OF KANSAS, THE EASTERN DISTRICT OF SOUTH CAROLINA AND THE EASTERN DISTRICT OF VIRGINIA, AND ON PETITION FOR A WRIT OF CERTIORARI TO THE SUPREME COURT OF DELAWARE, RESPECTIVELY

MEMORANDUM BRIEF FOR APPELLANTS IN NOS. 1, 2 AND 3 AND FOR RESPONDENTS IN NO. 5 ON FURTHER REARGUMENT WITH RESPECT TO THE EFFECT OF THE COURT'S DECREE

HAROLD SOLWARE,
ROBERT L. CARTER,
JACK GREENBERG,
OLIVER W. HILL,
THURGOOD MARSHALL,
LOUIS L. REDDING,
SPOTTSWOOD W. ROBINSON, III,
CHARLES S. SCOTT,
Attorneys for Appellants in Nos. 1, 2, 3 and for Respondents in No. 5.

CHARLES L. BLACK, JR.,
ELWOOD H. CHISOLM,
WILLIAM T. COLEMAN, JR.,
CHARLES T. DUNCAN,
GEORGE E. C. HAYES,
LORIN MILLER,
WILLIAM R. King, JR.,
CONSTANCE BAKER MOTLEY,
JAMES M. NABRIT, JR.,
LOUIS H. POLLAK,
FRANK D. REEVES,
JOHN SCOTT,
JACK B. WEINSTEIN,
of Counsel.

Oliver Brown was not the only African American who took the issue of segregated schools to the Supreme Court. He was joined in his case by four other suits from other parts of the country, shown here in this memorandum brief. But because the Brown case was listed first, their joint case was called Brown *v.* Board of Education of Topeka.

Thurgood Marshall was one of the NAACP lawyers who argued the Brown *case before the Supreme Court. Called "Mr. Civil Rights" for his heroic efforts to end segregation, Marshall argued 32 cases before the Supreme Court, winning 29. In 1967 he became the first African American appointed to the Supreme Court.*

Brown v. Board of Education of Topeka

(MAY 17, 1954)

It was the law in 17 southern and border states that African-American and white children attend separate public schools. Four other states segregated students by school districts. All these states justified their policy by saying that black and white schools were "separate but equal." According to an 1896 Supreme Court decision, *Plessy* v. *Ferguson*, separate facilities for African Americans and whites were legal if the facilities for both were equal. In 1954 the National Association for the Advancement of Colored People (NAACP) challenged the "separate but equal" doctrine at the elementary school level. NAACP lawyers argued before the Supreme Court that children in all-white schools received a better education than children in all-black schools. In May 1954 the Court agreed and outlawed racial segregation in public schools. Because of the *Brown* decision, African-American and white children, as well as children of all other races and ethnicities, today attend the same public schools.

These cases come to us from the states of Kansas, South Carolina, Virginia, and Delaware. They are premised on different facts and different local conditions, but a common legal question justifies their consideration together in this consolidated opinion.

In each of the cases, minors of the Negro race, through their legal representatives, seek the aid of the courts in obtaining admission to the public schools of their community on a nonsegregated basis. In each instance, they have been denied admission to schools attended by white children under laws requiring or permitting segregation according to race. This segregation was alleged to deprive the plaintiffs of the equal protection of the laws under the Fourteenth Amendment. In each of the cases other than the Delaware case, a three-judge federal district court denied relief to the plaintiffs on the so-called "separate but equal" doctrine announced by this Court in *Plessy* v. *Ferguson* [famous 1896 decision that declared social segregation of whites and blacks was legal]. . . . Under that doctrine, equality of treatment is accorded when the races are provided substantially equal facilities, even though these facilities be separate. . . .

The plaintiffs contend that segregated public schools are not "equal" and cannot be made "equal," and that hence they are deprived of the equal protection of the laws. Because of the obvious importance of the question presented, the Court took jurisdiction. . . .

There are findings below that the Negro and white schools involved have been equalized, or are being equalized, with respect to buildings, curricula, qualifications, and salaries of teachers, and other "tangible" factors. Our decision, therefore, cannot turn on merely a comparison of these tangible factors in the Negro and white schools involved in each of the cases. We must look instead to the effect of segregation itself on public education.

In approaching this problem, we cannot turn the clock back to 1868 when the Amendment was adopted, or even to 1896 when *Plessy* v. *Ferguson* was written. We must consider public education in the light of its full development and its present place in American life throughout the nation. Only in this way

The Brown in the case was Oliver Brown. He lived in Topeka, Kansas, which had segregated schools. Brown was angry that his eight-year-old daughter had to travel by bus to a black school even though the family lived only three blocks from an all-white public school.

In 1957 President Dwight Eisenhower called out federal troops to protect African-American students attempting to attend previously all-white Central High School in Little Rock, Arkansas. Angry white students are shown here shouting at and insulting Elizabeth Eckford.

Justice Earl Warren felt that the decision would have a more powerful effect if all the judges agreed. But two judges held out. Warren used all his political skills on them, and the final decision was unanimous.

can it be determined if segregation in public schools deprives these plaintiffs of the equal protection of the laws.

Today, education is perhaps the most important function of state and local governments. Compulsory school attendance laws and the great expenditures for education both demonstrate our recognition of the importance of education to our democratic society. It is required in the performance of our most basic public responsibilities, even service in the armed forces. It is the very foundation of good citizenship. Today it is a principal instrument in awakening the child to cultural values, in preparing him for later professional training, and in helping him to adjust normally to his environment. In these days, it is doubtful that any child may reasonably be expected to succeed in life if he is denied the opportunity of an education. Such an opportunity, where the state has undertaken to provide it, is a right which must be made available to all on equal terms.

We come then to the question presented: Does segregation of children in public schools solely on the basis of race, even though the physical facilities and other "tangible" factors may be equal, deprive the children of the minority group of equal educational opportunities? We believe that it does. . . .

To separate them from others of similar age and qualifications solely because of their race generates a feeling of inferiority as to their status in the community that may affect their hearts and minds in a way unlikely ever to be undone. The effect of this separation on their educational opportunities was well stated by a finding in the Kansas case by a court which nevertheless felt compelled to rule against the Negro plaintiffs:

"Segregation of white and colored children in public schools has a detrimental effect upon the colored children. The impact is greater when it has the sanction of the law; for the policy of separating the races is usually interpreted as denoting the inferiority of the Negro group. A sense of inferiority affects the motivation of a child to learn. Segregation with the sanction of law, therefore, has a tendency to retard the educational and mental development of Negro children and to deprive them of some of the benefits they would receive in a racially integrated school system."

Whatever may have been the extent of psychological knowledge at the time of *Plessy* v. *Ferguson*, this finding is amply supported by modern authority. Any language in Plessy *v.* Ferguson contrary to this finding is rejected.

We conclude that in the field of public education the doctrine of "separate but equal" has no place. Separate educational facilities are inherently unequal. Therefore, we hold that the plaintiffs and others similarly situated for whom the actions have been brought are, by reason of the segregation complained of, deprived of the equal protection of the laws guaranteed by the Fourteenth Amendment. . . .

The decision showed that people could bring cases into federal courts to fight racial segregation in all areas of American society.

AUTHOR

Earl Warren (1891–1974) was the fourteenth chief justice of the Supreme Court. A three-term governor of California, Warren was appointed chief justice by President Dwight D. Eisenhower in 1953. Warren proved to be a forceful leader. The Warren Court's decisions moved the nation closer to racial and social equality. This made him controversial. Many Americans applauded him, and Justice William O. Douglas called him "one of our three greatest Chief Justices." But some critics said he was too liberal and tried unsuccessfully to remove him from his position. In 1969 Earl Warren retired from the Court.

Six African-American teens who had attended Little Rock's Central High School in 1957–1958 sit with NAACP chief counsel Thurgood Marshall and Arkansas NAACP president Daisy Lee Gatson Bates outside the Supreme Court in this August 22, 1958, photo. From left to right are Melva Patillo, 16; Jefferson Thomas, 15; Gloria Ray, 15; Mrs. Bates; Thurgood Marshall; Carlotta Walls, 15; Minnie Jean Brown, 16; and Elizabeth Eckford, 16.

RESPONSE

African Americans praised the *Brown* decision, and many believed that school desegregation would be quick. They were wrong, although some school districts did integrate their students. Most southern states, however, refused to obey the ruling. So the next year the Supreme Court ordered the states to move forward "with all deliberate speed" to integrate their schools. Until the mid-1960s, federal judges had to push reluctant southern school districts and some northern schools to desegregate.

Inaugural Address

(JANUARY 20, 1961)

John F. Kennedy

President Dwight D. Eisenhower (right) with his successor, John F. Kennedy (left). They are shown here in top hats and overcoats as they prepare to leave the White House for the Capitol, where Kennedy was to take his oath of office.

Before a crowd shivering in 20°F temperature, forty-three-year-old John F. Kennedy stepped up to be sworn in as president of the United States. The youngest man to be elected president, he wore no coat or hat, as if to emphasize his youth and vitality. His inaugural address was a mere 1,350 words, brief for such speeches. It summarized his hopes for the nation. In the speech's most famous line, he called upon the American people to "ask not what your country can do for you—ask what you can do for your country." During his address, the new president made 77 changes in his reading copy. Although Kennedy later said he had been nervous, he spoke clearly and confidently. His speech energized the nation and inspired a generation of young Americans to find ways to serve their country.

The president-elect decided to make his address short. Explained Kennedy, "I don't want people to think I'm a windbag."

We observe today not a victory of party but a celebration of freedom—symbolizing an end as well as a beginning—signifying renewal as well as change. For I have sworn before you and Almighty God the same solemn oath our forebears prescribed nearly a century and three-quarters ago.

The world is very different now. For man holds in his mortal hands the power to abolish all forms of human poverty and all forms of human life. And yet the same revolutionary beliefs for which our forebears fought are still at issue around the globe—the belief that the rights of man come not from the generosity of the state but from the hand of God.

We dare not forget today that we are the heirs of that first revolution. Let the word go forth from this time and place, to friend and foe alike, that the torch has been passed to a new generation of Americans—born in this century, tempered by war, disciplined by a hard and bitter peace, proud of our ancient heritage—and unwilling to witness or permit the slow undoing of those human rights to which this nation has always been committed, and to which we are committed today at home and around the world.

Let every nation know, whether it wishes us well or ill, that we shall pay any price, bear any burden, meet any hardship, support any friend, oppose any foe to assure the survival and the success of liberty.

This much we pledge—and more.

To those old allies whose cultural and spiritual origins we share, we pledge the loyalty of faithful friends. United, there is little we cannot do in a host of cooperative ventures. Divided, there is little we can do—for we dare not meet a powerful challenge at odds and split asunder.

To those new states whom we welcome to the ranks of the free, we pledge our word that one form of colonial control shall not have passed away merely to be replaced by a far more iron tyranny. We shall not always expect to find them supporting our view. But we shall always hope to find them strongly supporting their own freedom—and to remember that, in the past, those who foolishly sought power by riding the back of the tiger ended up inside.

To those people in the huts and villages of half the globe

Kennedy asked his speechwriter to discover "the secret" of Lincoln's Gettysburg Address, which he hoped to use as a model. The speechwriter reported to him, "Lincoln never used a two- or three-syllable word where a one-syllable word would do, and never used two or three words where one word would do."

"No Kennedy speech," the speechwriter later recalled, "ever underwent so many drafts." Although the president asked his staff for suggestions, the end product was his own.

struggling to break the bonds of mass misery, we pledge our best efforts to help them help themselves, for whatever period is required—not because the Communists may be doing it, not because we seek their votes, but because it is right. If a free society cannot help the many who are poor, it cannot save the few who are rich.

To our sister republics south of the border, we offer a special pledge—to convert our good words into good deeds—in a new alliance for progress—to assist free men and free governments in casting off the chains of poverty. But this peaceful revolution of hope cannot become the prey of hostile powers. Let all our neighbors know that we shall join with them to oppose aggression or subversion anywhere in the Americas. And let every other power know that this hemisphere intends to remain the master of its own house.

To that world assembly of sovereign states, the United Nations, our last best hope in an age where the instruments of

President Kennedy plays in the Oval Office in 1962 with his two children, John Jr. and Caroline. Kennedy's administration brought a breath of youth and glamour to the presidency. John Jr. and Caroline were the youngest children of a president to live in the White House in more than 60 years.

war have far outpaced the instruments of peace, we renew our pledge of support—to prevent it from becoming merely a forum for invective—to strengthen its shield of the new and the weak—and to enlarge the area in which its writ may run.

Finally, to those nations who would make themselves our adversary, we offer not a pledge but a request: that both sides begin anew the quest for peace, before the dark powers of destruction unleashed by science engulf all humanity in planned or accidental self-destruction.

We dare not tempt them with weakness. For only when our arms are sufficient beyond doubt can we be certain beyond doubt that they will never be employed.

But neither can two great and powerful groups of nations take comfort from our present course—both sides overburdened by the cost of modern weapons, both rightly alarmed by the steady spread of the deadly atom, yet both racing to alter that uncertain balance of terror that stays the hand of mankind's final war.

So let us begin anew—remembering on both sides that civility is not a sign of weakness, and sincerity is always subject to proof. Let us never negotiate out of fear. But let us never fear to negotiate.

Let both sides explore what problems unite us instead of belaboring those problems which divide us.

Let both sides, for the first time, formulate serious and precise proposals for the inspection and control of arms—and bring the absolute power to destroy other nations under the absolute control of all nations.

Let both sides seek to invoke the wonders of science instead of its terrors. Together let us explore the stars, conquer the deserts, eradicate disease, tap the ocean depths, and encourage the arts and commerce.

Let both sides unite to heed in all corners of the earth the command of Isaiah—to "undo the heavy burdens . . .[and] let the oppressed go free."

And if a beachhead of cooperation may push back the jungle of suspicion, let both sides join in creating a new endeavor, not a new balance of power, but a new world of law, where the strong are just and the weak secure and the peace preserved.

The morning of his inauguration Kennedy arose early and, in between bites of breakfast, practiced the speech aloud to make it sound just right.

All this will not be finished in the first one hundred days. Nor will it be finished in the first one thousand days, nor in the life of this administration, nor even perhaps in our lifetime on this planet. But let us begin.

In your hands, my fellow citizens, more than mine, will rest the final success or failure of our course. Since this country was founded, each generation of Americans has been summoned to give testimony to its national loyalty. The graves of young Americans who answered the call to service surround the globe.

Now the trumpet summons us again—not as a call to bear arms, though arms we need,—not as a call to battle, though embattled we are—but a call to bear the burden of a long twilight struggle, year in and year out, "rejoicing in hope, patient in tribulation"—a struggle against the common enemies of man: tyranny, poverty, disease, and war itself.

Can we forge against these enemies a grand and global alliance, North and South, East and West, that can assure a more fruitful life for all mankind? Will you join in that historic effort?

In the long history of the world, only a few generations have been granted the role of defending freedom in its hour of maximum danger. I do not shrink from this responsibility—I welcome it. I do not believe that any of us would exchange places with any other people or any other generation. The energy, the faith, the devotion which we bring to this endeavor will light our country and all who serve it—and the glow from that fire can truly light the world.

And so, my fellow Americans: ask not what your country can do for you—ask what you can do for your country.

My fellow citizens of the world: ask not what America will do for you, but what together we can do for the freedom of man.

Finally, whether you are citizens of America or citizens of the world, ask of us here the same high standards of strength and sacrifice which we ask of you. With a good conscience our only sure reward, with history the final judge of our deeds, let us go forth to lead the land we love, asking His blessing and His help, but knowing that here on earth God's work must truly be our own.

John Fitzgerald Kennedy took the oath of office as the thirty-fifth president of the United States on January 20, 1961. Although Kennedy was the youngest man elected president, he was not the youngest president in American history. Vice President Theodore Roosevelt was 279 days younger than Kennedy when he became president after the assassination of President William McKinley.

AUTHOR

John F. Kennedy (1917–1963) was the thirty-fifth president. Born into a wealthy Massachusetts Irish-American family, he was the first Catholic ever elected president. In the closest election since 1884, the Democratic senator from Massachusetts squeaked past Republican Vice President Richard Nixon by only 100,000 votes. During the campaign Kennedy promised voters a "New Frontier." His New Frontier included such programs as more federal aid to education and the institution of the Peace Corps to help poor people around the world.

But once in office, Kennedy had a hard time getting Congress to support his goals. Many New Frontier programs were not passed because of the opposition of conservative southern Democrats in Congress who thought his goals were too liberal. Yet some New Frontier programs were enacted. One of the most popular, the Peace Corps, sent thousands of volunteers—mostly young people—to help in underdeveloped countries. Kennedy's term was cut short when he was assassinated in Dallas by Lee Harvey Oswald on November 23, 1963.

RESPONSE

Americans were captivated by the image of the young, handsome, dynamic president. Around the world, his speech won praise for its moderate tone. Even America's Cold War enemy, the Soviet Union, did not react to it with hostility.

THE DECLARATION OF INDIAN PURPOSE

(JUNE 20, 1961)

In 1969 Native American activists occupied the former prison island of Alcatraz, in San Francisco's harbor. This photograph shows some of them standing under signs they painted to express their message.

In June 1961 Native American activists met at a nationwide Indian Conference in Chicago. The delegates drafted a Declaration of Indian Purpose to protest the government's termination policy. This policy, begun in 1953, allowed Congress to terminate a tribe by making a law saying that the tribe no longer legally or politically existed. Between 1954 and 1962 Congress terminated more than 60 tribes, most of them in the West. The delegates felt that the termination policy was a way of exploiting Indian lands. The declaration asked Congress to change course completely. Rather than disbanding tribes, the federal government was asked to help Native Americans preserve and develop their own communities.

Anger over the policy launched a Native American movement to defend Indian rights. In a series of decisions, the Supreme Court returned a large part of tribal independence, lands, and artifacts. This process continues today. The following passage is from the declaration.

STATEMENT OF PURPOSE:

. . . In order to give recognition to certain basic philosophies by which the Indian People live, We, the Indian People, must be governed by principles in a democratic manner with a right to choose our way of life. Since our Indian culture is threatened by presumption of being absorbed by the American society, we believe we have the responsibility of preserving our precious heritage. We believe that the Indians must provide the adjustment and thus freely advance with dignity to a better life. . . .

CREED:

We believe in the inherent right of all people to retain spiritual and cultural values, and that the free exercise of these values is necessary to the normal development of any people. Indians exercised this inherent right to live their own lives for thousands of years before the white man came and took their lands. It is a more complex world in which Indians live today, but the Indian people who first settled the New World and built the great civilizations which only now are being dug out of the past, long ago demonstrated that they could master complexity.

We believe that the history and development of America show that the Indian has been subjected to duress, undue influence, unwarranted pressures, and policies which have produced uncertainty, frustration, and despair. Only when the public understands these conditions and is moved to take action toward the formulation and adoption of sound and consistent policies and programs will these destroying factors be removed and the Indian resume his normal growth and make his maximum contribution to modern society.

We believe in the future of a greater America, an America which we were first to love, where life, liberty, and the pursuit of happiness will be a reality. In such a future, with Indians and all other Americans cooperating, a cultural climate will be created in which the Indian people will grow and develop as members of a free society.

CONCLUDING STATEMENT:

To complete our Declaration, we point out that in the beginning the people of the New World, called Indians by accident of

Non-Indians could attend some meetings of the conference, but only as silent observers.

geography, were possessed of a continent and a way of life. In the course of many lifetimes, our people had adjusted to every climate and condition from the Arctic to the torrid zones. In their livelihood and family relationships, their ceremonial observances, they reflected the diversity of the physical world they occupied.

The conditions in which Indians live today reflect a world in which every basic aspect of life has been transformed. Even the physical world is no longer the controlling factor in determining where and under what conditions men may live. In region after region, Indian groups found their means of existence either totally destroyed or materially modified. Newly introduced diseases swept away or reduced regional populations. These changes were followed by major shifts in the internal life of tribe and family.

The time came when the Indian people were no longer the masters of their situation. Their life ways survived subject to the will of a dominant sovereign power. This is said, not in a spirit of complaint; we understand that in the lives of all nations of people, there are times of plenty and times of famine. But we do speak out in a plea for understanding.

When we go before the American people, as we do in this Declaration, and ask for material assistance in developing our resources and developing our opportunities, we pose a moral problem which cannot be left unanswered. For the problem we raise affects the standing which our nation sustains before world opinion.

Our situation cannot be relieved by appropriated funds alone, though it is equally obvious that without capital investment and funded services, solutions will be delayed. Nor will the passage of time lessen the complexities which beset a people moving toward new meaning and purpose.

The answers we seek are not commodities to be purchased, neither are they evolved automatically through the passing of time.

The effort to place social adjustment on a money-time interval scale which has characterized Indian administration, has resulted in unwanted pressure and frustration.

When Indians speak of the continent they yielded, they are

The government made onetime payments to terminated tribes in exchange for their lands. These payments were divided among the members of the former tribes. For the most part, these payments were small and many Indians had to take low-paying jobs or depend on government services to survive.

not referring only to the loss of some millions of acres in real estate. They have in mind that the land supported a universe of things they knew, valued, and loved.

With that continent gone, except for the few poor parcels they still retain, the basis of life is precariously held, but they mean to hold the scraps and parcels as earnestly as any small nation or ethnic group was ever determined to hold to identity and survival.

What we ask of America is not charity, not paternalism, even when benevolent. We ask only that the nature of our situation be recognized and made the basis of policy and action.

In short, the Indians ask for assistance, technical and financial, for the time needed, however long that may be, to regain in the America of the space age some measure of the adjustment they enjoyed as the original possessors of their native land.

One Indian wept as his tribe signed a contract giving the tribe's best land in North Dakota to the government. He said, "The members of the tribal council sign this contract with heavy hearts."

AUTHORS

About 700 Indians from 64 tribes took part in the congress. They drafted, debated, and passed the Declaration of Indian Purpose.

RESPONSE

The delegates made themselves heard. By the early 1960s, the government ended its termination policy.

In 1973 Native American militants took control of the village at Wounded Knee, South Dakota. This photograph shows them surrounding a car carrying the assistant attorney general from a meeting with militant leaders.

SILENT SPRING

(1962)

RACHEL CARSON

After Rachel Carson published Silent Spring, *President Kennedy requested a report on pesticides from the scientists who advised his administration. Their report agreed with Carson and suggested ways to control the use of pesticides.*

Since World War II, author and scientist Rachel Carson had worried about the insecticide DDT and its effects on humans, wildlife, and the earth's environment. Manufacturers were producing DDT and other poisonous pesticides, and people used them without thinking about the harm they might do. In *Silent Spring*, Carson eloquently voiced her concerns. *Silent Spring* was one of the most influential books in the second half of the twentieth century. It launched the environmental movement in the United States. Carson's book also alerted people worldwide to the dangers of industrial environmental pollution. The following passage is from *Silent Spring*.

. . . It took hundreds of millions of years to produce the life that now inhabits the earth—eons of time in which that developing and evolving and diversifying life reached a state of adjustment and balance with its surroundings. The environment, rigorously shaping and directing the life it supported, contained elements that were hostile as well as supporting. Certain rocks gave out dangerous radiation; even within the light of the sun, from which all life draws its energy, there were short-wave radiations with power to injure. Given time—time not in years, but in millennia—life adjusts, and a balance has been reached. For time is the essential ingredient; but in the modern world there is no time.

The rapidity of change and the speed with which new situations are created follow the impetuous and heedless pace of man rather than the deliberate pace of nature. Radiation is no longer merely the background radiation of rocks, the bombardment of cosmic rays, the ultraviolet of the sun that have existed before there was any life on earth; radiation is now the unnatural creation of man's tampering with the atom. The chemicals to which life is asked to make its adjustment are no longer merely the calcium and silica and copper and all the rest of the minerals washed out of the rocks and carried in rivers to the sea; they are the synthetic creations of man's inventive mind, brewed in his laboratories, and having no counterparts in nature.

To adjust to these chemicals would require time on the scale that is nature's; it would require not merely the years of a man's life but the life of generations. And even this, were it by some miracle possible, would be futile, for the new chemicals come from our laboratories in an endless stream; almost five hundred annually find their way into actual use in the United States alone. The figure is staggering and its implications are not easily grasped—500 new chemicals to which the bodies of men and animals are required somehow to adapt each year, chemicals totally outside the limits of biologic experience.

Among them are many that are used in man's war against nature. Since the mid-1940's over 200 basic chemicals have been created for use in killing insects, weeds, rodents, and other organisms described in the modern vernacular as "pests"; and

In 1951 Carson published The Sea Around Us, *which described the history, chemistry, biology, and ecology of the sea. This book, which was translated into many languages, made her famous. In all her writings, she emphasized the interrelation of living things and how the welfare of humans depends on the welfare of all the natural world. An editor said about Rachel Carson, "A few thousand words from her and the world took a new direction."*

they are sold under several thousand different brand names.

These sprays, dusts, and aerosols are now applied almost universally to farms, gardens, forests, and homes—nonselective chemicals that have the power to kill every insect, the "good" and the "bad," to still the song of birds and the leaping of fish in the streams, to coat the leaves with a deadly film, and to linger on in the soil—all this though the intended target may be only a few weeds or insects. Can anyone believe it is possible to lay down such a barrage of poisons on the surface of the earth without making it unfit for all life? They should not be called "insecticides," but "biocides."

The whole process of spraying seems caught up in an endless spiral. Since DDT was released for civilian use, a process of escalation has been going on in which ever more toxic materials must be found. This has happened because insects, in a triumphant vindication of Darwin's principle of the survival of the fittest, have evolved super races immune to the particular insecticide used, hence a deadlier one has always to be developed—and then a deadlier one than that. . . .

The "control of nature" is a phrase conceived in arrogance, born of the Neanderthal age of biology and philosophy, when it was supposed that nature exists for the convenience of man. The concepts and practices of applied entomology for the most part date from that Stone Age of science. It is our alarming misfortune that so primitive a science has armed itself with the most modern and terrible weapons, and that in turning them against the insects it has also turned them against the earth.

A condensed version of Silent Spring *was printed in* The New Yorker *magazine in June 1962. While many scientists and chemical companies responded with outrage, some readers paid close attention to Carson's warning about the dangers of chemical pesticides. President Kennedy ordered a study on the effects of pesticides and Congressman John Lindsay inserted portions of the* New Yorker *article into the* Congressional Record.

AUTHOR

Rachel Carson (1907–1964) was a biologist and writer. Born in Pennsylvania, her childhood interest in wildlife led Carson to attend Johns Hopkins University. She taught zoology at the University at Maryland until 1936. Carson then went to work for many years as a marine biologist for the United States government.

RESPONSE

Silent Spring became a best-seller. The agricultural and chemical industries, however, were infuriated by what they saw as an attack against their practices. They struck back, blasting the book and throwing their support behind those who disagreed with Carson. Today, *Silent Spring* is recognized as one of the principal documents of the environmental movement. It helped lead to the formation of the Environmental Protection Agency (EPA) in 1970 and to the ban on DDT in 1972. Vice President Al Gore said Carson brought to light "what is arguably the most important issue of our era."

Crop-dusting planes sprayed pesticides over acres of land. Because of the harmful effects of poisonous pesticides such as DDT, new insecticides have been developed that control pests while causing minimum damage to the environment.

Carson once wrote, "The beauty of the living world I was trying to save has always been uppermost in my mind. . . . Now I can believe I have at least helped a little."

SPEECH AT THE BERLIN WALL

(JUNE 26, 1963)

JOHN F. KENNEDY

Two months before he spoke at the Berlin Wall, President Kennedy began to think about ways of easing the Cold War. He said that both sides had been "caught up in a vicious cycle in which suspicion on one side breeds suspicion on the other."

After World War II, the German city of Berlin was divided. The Soviets controlled East Berlin, while England, France, and the United States controlled West Berlin. In August 1961 the Russians suddenly closed the border between East and West Berlin. They also built a concrete-and-barbed-wire wall to stop East Germans from fleeing to the West. But people kept on trying anyway; some even died in the attempt. Two years later, President John F. Kennedy made a speech at the wall. To show his support for the people of Berlin, he proclaimed, "Ich bin ein Berliner."

Kennedy's speech by the Berlin Wall is considered one of his best. Little did he or his listeners know that 28 years later, the Communist East German government would open the wall to stop its people from fleeing to Czechoslovakia. Later in that same year, Communist governments across Eastern Europe fell. The German people tore the wall completely down. The demolition of the Berlin Wall came to symbolize the end of Communist power in Europe. The Cold War was over.

President John F. Kennedy addresses a crowd of more than 300,000 West Berliners at Schoneberg Town, proudly proclaiming "Ich bin ein Berliner." *Although the German translation means "I am a doughnut" in local slang, and Kennedy was trying to say, "I am a Berliner," the crowd cheered his efforts anyway.*

The Soviets erected the Berlin Wall to stop the large exodus of people fleeing East Berlin for the non-Communist world. Between 1949 and July 1961 at least 2.7 million people fled East Germany, many of them through West Berlin.

Two thousand years ago the proudest boast was "Civitas Romanus sum." ["I am a Roman citizen."] Today, in the world of freedom, the proudest boast is *"Ich bin ein Berliner."*

There are many people in the world who really don't understand, or say they don't, what is the great issue between the free world and the Communist world. Let them come to Berlin. There are some who say that Communism is the wave of the future. Let them come to Berlin. And there are some who say in Europe and elsewhere we can work with the Communists. Let them come to Berlin. And there are even a few who say that it is true that Communism is an evil system, but it permits us to make economic progress. *"Lasst sie nach Berlin kommen."* ["Let them come to Berlin."]

Freedom has many difficulties and democracy is not perfect, but we have never had to put a wall up to keep our people in,

Around the time Kennedy spoke at the Berlin Wall, the Americans and Soviets set up a telephone hotline so that leaders of each country could speak directly to each other during any crises, hoping to avert unnecessary hostilities.

to prevent them from leaving us. I want to say, on behalf of my countrymen, who live many miles away on the other side of the Atlantic, who are far distant from you, that they take the greatest pride that they have been able to share with you, even from a distance, the story of the last eighteen years. I know of no town, no city, that has been besieged for eighteen years that still lives with the vitality and the force, and the hope and the determination of the city of West Berlin. While the wall is the most obvious and vivid demonstration of the failures of the Communist system, for all the world to see, we take no satisfaction in it, for it is an offense not only against history but an offense against humanity, separating families, dividing husbands and wives and brothers and sisters, and dividing a people who wish to be joined together.

What is true of this city is true of Germany—real, lasting peace in Europe can never be assured as long as one German out of four is denied the elementary right of free men, and that is to make a free choice. In eighteen years of peace and good faith, this generation of Germans has earned the right to be free, including the right to unite their families and their nation in lasting peace with good will to all people. You live in a defended island of freedom, but your life is part of the main. So let me ask you, as I close, to lift your eyes beyond the dangers of today to the hopes of tomorrow, beyond the freedom merely of this city of Berlin, or your country of Germany, to the advance of freedom everywhere, beyond the wall to the day of peace with justice, beyond yourselves and ourselves to all mankind. Freedom is indivisible, and when one man is enslaved, all are not free. When all are free, then we can look forward to that day when this city will be joined as one—and this country, and this great continent of Europe—in a peaceful and hopeful glow. When that day finally comes, as it will, the people of West Berlin can take sober satisfaction in the fact that they were in the front lines for almost two decades.

All free men, wherever they may live, are citizens of Berlin, and therefore, as a free man, I take pride in the words *"Ich bin ein Berliner."*

AUTHOR

Throughout his presidency, John F. Kennedy dealt with Cold War tensions between the United States and the Soviet Union. In April 1961 he supported an unsuccessful attempt by exiled Cubans to overthrow the Communist government in Cuba. The next year, worried that the Soviets were stockpiling missiles in Cuba, he demanded that they be removed. The Soviets backed down and shipped the missiles back to Russia. During Kennedy's term, he also sent more American advisers to Asia, particularly to Vietnam to help save the anti-Communist government of South Vietnam, which was engaged in a civil war with Vietnamese Communists known as the Vietcong. On November 22, 1963, Kennedy was assassinated in Dallas, Texas. Vice President Lyndon B. Johnson succeeded him. Johnson's Great Society program put into effect many social reforms, some of which had been proposed by John F. Kennedy.

RESPONSE

The Western powers hailed President Kennedy's speech, as did the American people and the media.

This photograph shows Kennedy touring Checkpoint Charlie, the main crossing point from East to West Berlin and back, maintained by United States forces.

With an estimated crowd of 250,000, the March on Washington was, according to King, "the greatest demonstration of freedom in the history of our nation."

THE MARCH ON WASHINGTON ADDRESS

(AUGUST 28, 1963)

MARTIN LUTHER KING, JR.

As summer 1963 drew to a close, a huge crowd made up of Americans from all walks of life gathered at the Lincoln Memorial to rally for jobs and racial justice. At the end of a day of stirring songs and speeches, Martin Luther King, Jr., rose to speak. Although he gave many eloquent speeches during his life, the March on Washington Address was one of King's most memorable. It summed up the hopes and dreams of the civil rights movement, which sought to end segregation and bring true equality to black Americans. Many Americans today instantly recognize the speech's most famous line, "I have a dream."

Five score years ago, a great American, in whose symbolic shadow we stand, signed the Emancipation Proclamation. This momentous decree came as a great beacon light of hope to millions of Negro slaves who had been seared in the flames of withering injustice. It came as a joyous daybreak to end the long night of captivity.

But one hundred years later, we must face the tragic fact that the Negro is still not free. One hundred years later, the life of the Negro is still sadly crippled by the manacles of segregation and the chains of discrimination. One hundred years later, the Negro lives on a lonely island of poverty in the midst of a vast ocean of material prosperity. One hundred years later, the Negro is still languishing in the corners of American society and finds himself an exile in his own land. So we have come here today to dramatize an appalling condition.

In a sense we have come to our nation's Capital to cash a check. When the architects of our republic wrote the magnificent words of the Constitution and the Declaration of Independence, they were signing a promissory note to which every American fell heir. This note was a promise that all men would be guaranteed the unalienable rights of life, liberty, and the pursuit of happiness.

It is obvious today that America has defaulted on this promissory note insofar as her citizens of color are concerned. Instead of honoring this sacred obligation, America has given the Negro people a bad check; a check which has come back marked "insufficient funds." But we refuse to believe that the bank of justice is bankrupt. We refuse to believe that there are insufficient funds in the great vaults of opportunity of this nation. So we have come to cash this check—a check that will give us upon demand the riches of freedom and the security of justice.

We have also come to this hallowed spot to remind America of the fierce urgency of *now*. This is not time to engage in the luxury of cooling off or to take the tranquilizing drug of gradualism. *Now* is the time to make real the promises of democracy. *Now* is the time to rise from the dark and desolate valley of segregation to the sunlit path of racial justice. Now is the time to open the doors of opportunity to all of God's children. *Now* is

In the crowd that day at the Lincoln Memorial, about 50,000 listeners were white.

Civil rights leaders met with President Kennedy on the day of the 1963 March on Washington. Martin Luther King, Jr., is the second person from the left.

The African-American spiritual "We Shall Overcome" was the anthem of the civil rights movement. Earlier during the rally, folksinger Joan Baez led the huge crowd in joining hands and singing it.

the time to lift our nation from the quicksands of racial injustice to the solid rock of brotherhood.

It would be fatal for the nation to overlook the urgency of the moment and to underestimate the determination of the Negro. This sweltering summer of the Negro's legitimate discontent will not pass until there is an invigorating autumn of freedom and equality. Nineteen sixty-three is not an end, but a beginning. Those who hope that the Negro needed to blow off steam and will now be content will have a rude awakening if the nation returns to business as usual. There will be neither rest nor tranquillity in America until the Negro is granted his citizenship rights. The whirlwinds of revolt will continue to shake the foundations of our nation until the bright day of justice emerges.

But there is something that I must say to my people who stand on the warm threshold which leads into the palace of justice. In the process of gaining our rightful place we must not be guilty of wrongful deeds. Let us not seek to satisfy our thirst for freedom by drinking from the cup of bitterness and hatred. We must forever conduct our struggle on the high plane of dignity and discipline. We must not allow our creative protest to degenerate into physical violence. Again and again we must rise to the majestic heights of meeting physical force with soul force.

The marvelous new militancy which has engulfed the Negro community must not lead us to a distrust of all white people, for many of our white brothers, as evidenced by their presence here today, have come to realize that their freedom is inextricably bound to our freedom. We cannot walk alone.

And as we walk, we must make the pledge that we shall march ahead. We cannot turn back. There are those who are asking the devotees of civil rights, "When will you be satisfied?"

We can never be satisfied as long as the Negro is the victim of the unspeakable horrors of police brutality.

We can never be satisfied as long as our bodies, heavy with fatigue of travel, cannot gain lodging in the motels of the highways and the cities.

We cannot be satisfied as long as the Negro's basic mobility is from a smaller ghetto to a larger one.

We can never be satisfied as long as a Negro in Mississippi

cannot vote and a Negro in New York believes he has nothing for which to vote.

No, no, we are not satisfied, and we will not be satisfied until justice rolls down like waters and righteousness like a mighty stream.

I am not unmindful that some of you have come here out of great trials and tribulations. Some of you have come fresh from narrow jail cells. Some of you have come from areas where your quest for freedom left you battered by the storms of persecution and staggered by the winds of police brutality. You have been the veterans of creative suffering. Continue to work with the faith that unearned suffering is redemptive.

Go back to Mississippi, go back to Alabama, go back to South Carolina, go back to Georgia, go back to Louisiana, go back to the slums and ghettos of our Northern cities, knowing that somehow this situation can and will be changed. Let us not wallow in the valley of despair.

I say to you today, my friends, that in spite of the difficulties and frustrations of the moment I still have a dream. It is a dream deeply rooted in the American dream.

I have a dream that one day this nation will rise up and live out the true meaning of its creed: "We hold these truths to be self-evident; that all men are created equal."

I have a dream that one day on the red hills of Georgia the sons of former slaves and the sons of former slaveowners will be able to sit down together at the table of brotherhood.

I have a dream that one day even the state of Mississippi, a desert state sweltering with the heat of injustice and oppression, will be transformed into an oasis of freedom and justice.

I have a dream that my four little children will one day live in a nation where they will not be judged by the color of their skin but by the content of their character.

I have a dream today.

I have a dream that one day the state of Alabama, whose governor's lips are presently dripping with the words of interposition and nullification, will be transformed into a situation where little black boys and black girls will be able to join hands with little white boys and girls and walk together as sisters and brothers.

On April 3, King made a speech in Memphis in which he seemed to foresee his own death. King said, "We've got some difficult days ahead, but it really doesn't matter to me now, because I've been to the mountaintop." The next evening a sniper killed him while he stood on his motel balcony.

I have a dream today.

I have a dream that one day every valley shall be exalted, every hill and mountain shall be made low, the rough places will be made plain, and the crooked places will be made straight, and the glory of the Lord shall be revealed, and all flesh shall see it together.

This is our hope. This is the faith with which I return to the South. With this faith we will be able to hew out of the mountain of despair a stone of hope. With this faith we will be able to transform the jangling discords of our nation into a beautiful symphony of brotherhood.

With this faith we will be able to work together, to pray together, to struggle together, to go to jail together, to stand up for freedom together, knowing that we will be free one day.

This will be the day when all of God's children will be able to sing with new meaning, "My country 'tis of thee, sweet land of liberty, of thee I sing. Land where my father died, land of the Pilgrims' pride, from every mountainside, let freedom ring."

And if America is to be a great nation, this must become true. So let freedom ring from the prodigious hilltops of New Hampshire. Let freedom ring from the mighty mountains of New York. Let freedom ring from the heightening Alleghenies of Pennsylvania!

Let freedom ring from the snowcapped Rockies of Colorado! Let freedom ring from the curvaceous peaks of California! But not only that; let freedom ring from Stone Mountain of Georgia! Let freedom ring from Lookout Mountain of Tennessee!

Let freedom ring from every hill and molehill of Mississippi. From every mountainside, let freedom ring.

When we let freedom ring, when we let it ring from every village and every hamlet, from every state and every city, we will be able to speed up that day when all of God's children, black men and white men, Jews and Gentiles, Protestants and Catholics, will be able to join hands and sing in the words of the old Negro spiritual, "Free at last! Free at last! Thank God Almighty, we are free at last!"

AUTHOR

In the years following the "I Have a Dream" speech, Martin Luther King, Jr., remained committed to nonviolence, despite mounting criticism inside the civil rights movement. He also widened his interests. In early 1968 he began a "Poor People's Campaign" to deal with economic problems, and he spoke out against American involvement in the Vietnam War. On April 4, 1968, while in Memphis, Tennessee, to support striking sanitation workers, King was assassinated. His birthday, January 15, has become a national holiday.

RESPONSE

The "I Have a Dream" speech was seen by live television audiences throughout the United States. In October 1963 Congress began deliberating on the Civil Rights Act. The bill, which passed in 1964, ended segregation in public places such as lunch counters and hotels and outlawed discrimination in employment by race, color, sex, religion, or national origin. It also gave the government the power to sue to desegregate public places such as museums and schools.

Martin Luther King, Jr., made up the most famous part of his speech as he was speaking to the thousands who had gathered to hear him at the Lincoln Memorial in Washington, D.C.

The Ballot or The Bullet

(APRIL 3, 1964)

Malcolm X

Malcolm X is shown here in May 1963 addressing a Harlem rally in support of integration efforts in Birmingham, Alabama. Malcolm X wrote, "The black race here in North America is in extremely bad condition. You show me a black man who isn't an extremist, and I'll show you one who needs psychiatric attention."

Some civil rights workers grew impatient with Martin Luther King, Jr.'s tactics of nonviolent civil disobedience. They urged African Americans to take control of their own communities and to rely on direct action and self-defense. Malcolm X was the most forceful voice of what became known as the Black Power movement. In early April, he spoke before the Congress of Racial Equality (CORE), an important civil rights organization. Malcolm X warned there would be another kind of march on Washington if Congress delayed passing civil rights legislation. This compelling speech with its message of black pride has helped make Malcolm X a hero to many Americans.

So, what I'm trying to impress upon you, in essence, is this: You and I in America are faced not with a segregationist conspiracy, we're faced with a government conspiracy. . . . You don't have anybody putting blocks in your path but people who are a part of the government. The same government that you go abroad to fight for and die for is the government that is in a conspiracy to deprive you of your voting rights, deprive you of your economic opportunities, deprive you of decent housing, deprive you of decent education. You don't need to go to the employer alone, it is the government itself, the government of America, that is responsible for the oppression and exploitation and degradation of black people in this country. And you should drop it in their lap. This government has failed the Negro. This so-called democracy has failed the Negro. And all these white liberals have definitely failed the Negro.

So where do we go from here? First, we need some friends. We need some new allies. The entire civil-rights struggle needs a new interpretation, a broader interpretation. We need to look at this civil-rights thing from another angle—from the inside as well as from the outside. To those of us whose philosophy is black nationalism, the only way you can get involved in the civil-rights struggle is give it a new interpretation. That old interpretation excluded us. It kept us out. So, we're giving a new interpretation to the civil-rights struggle, an interpretation that will enable us to come into it, take part in it. And these handkerchief-heads who have been dillydallying and pussyfooting and compromising—we don't intend to let them pussyfoot and dillydally and compromise any longer.

How can you thank a man for giving you what's already yours? How then can you thank him for giving you only part of what's already yours? You haven't even made progress, if what's being given to you, you should have had already. That's not progress. And I love my Brother Lomax [Louis Lomax, a leader of the civil rights group, the Congress of Racial Equality (CORE)], the way he pointed out we're right back where we were in 1954. We're behind where we were in 1954. We're not even as far up as we were in 1954. There's more segregation now than there was in 1954. There's more racial animosity, more racial hatred, more racial violence today in 1964, than

The X *in Malcolm X stood for the stolen identity of African slaves.*

there was in 1954. Where is the progress?

And now you're facing a situation where the young Negro's coming up. They don't want to hear that "turn-the-other-cheek" stuff, no. In Jacksonville, those were teenagers, they were throwing Molotov cocktails. Negroes have never done that before. But it shows you there's a new deal coming in. There's new thinking coming in. There's new strategy coming in. It'll be Molotov cocktails this month, hand grenades next month, and something else next month. It'll be ballots, or it'll be bullets. It'll be liberty, or it will be death. The only difference about this kind of death—it'll be reciprocal. You know what is meant by "reciprocal"? That's one of Brother Lomax's words, I stole it from him. I don't usually deal with those big words because I don't usually deal with big people. I deal with small people. I find you can get a whole lot of small people and whip hell out of a whole lot of big people. They haven't got anything to lose, and they've got everything to gain. And they'll let you know in a minute: "It takes two to tango; when I go, you go."

Malcolm X was a popular speaker on college campuses. Both white and African-American students flocked to hear his condemnation of "Whitism," or white supremacy.

Many young African Americans were impatient with the nonviolent tactics of Martin Luther King, Jr. These young people made up what came to be called the Black Power movement. This photograph shows teenagers and children lifting their fists in the Black Power salute outside their school in San Francisco in 1969.

The black nationalists, those whose philosophy is black nationalism, in bringing about this new interpretation of the entire meaning of civil rights, look upon it as meaning, as Brother Lomax has pointed out, equality of opportunity. Well, we're justified in seeking civil rights, if it means equality of opportunity, because all we're doing there is trying to collect for our investment. Our mothers and fathers invested sweat and blood. Three hundred and ten years we worked in this country without a dime in return—I mean without a *dime* in return. You let the white man walk around here talking about how rich this country is, but you never stop to think how it got rich so quick. It got rich because you made it rich.

You take the people who are in this audience right now. They're poor, we're all poor as individuals. Our weekly salary individually amounts to hardly anything. But if you take the salary of everyone in here collectively it'll fill up a whole lot of baskets. It's a lot of wealth. If you can collect the wages of just these people right here for a year, you'll be rich—richer than rich. When you look at it like that, think how rich Uncle Sam had to become, not with this handful, but millions of black people. Your and my mother and father, who didn't work an eight-hour shift, but worked from "can't see" in the morning until "can't see" at night, and worked for nothing, making the white man rich, making Uncle Sam rich.

This is our investment. This is our contribution—our blood. Not only did we give of our free labor, we gave of our blood. Every time he had a call to arms, we were the first ones in uniform. We died on every battlefield the white man had. We have made a greater sacrifice than anybody who's standing up in America today. We have made a greater contribution and have collected less. Civil rights, for those of us whose philosophy is black nationalism, means "Give it to us now. Don't wait for next year. Give it to us yesterday, and that's not fast enough.". . .

If you don't take this kind of stand, your little children will grow up and look at you and think "shame." If you don't take an uncompromising stand—I don't mean go out and get violent; but at the same time you should never be nonviolent unless you run into some nonviolence. I'm nonviolent with those who are nonviolent with me. But when you drop that vio-

After a 1964 pilgrimage to Mecca, the holy city of the Islamic religion, Malcolm X left behind his black separatist views and focused on accomplishing social change through community action.

lence on me, then you've made me go insane, and I'm not responsible for what I do. And that's the way every Negro should get. Any time you know you're within the law, within your legal rights, within your moral rights, in accord with justice, then die for what you believe in. But don't die alone. Let your dying be reciprocal. This is what is meant by equality. What's good for the goose is good for the gander. . . .

If a Negro in 1964 has to sit around and wait for some cracker [poor southern white] senator to filibuster when it comes to the rights of black people, why, you and I should hang our heads in shame. You talk about a march on Washington in 1963, you haven't seen anything. There's some more going down in '64. And this time they're not going like they went last year. They're not going singing "We Shall Overcome." They're not going with white friends. They're not going with placards already painted for them. They're not going with round-trip tickets. They're going with one-way tickets.

And if they don't want that nonviolent army going down there, tell them to bring the filibuster to a halt. The black nationalists aren't going to wait. Lyndon B. Johnson is the head of the Democratic Party. If he's for civil rights, let him go into the Senate next week and declare himself. Let him go in there right now and declare himself. Let him go in there and denounce the Southern branch of his party. Let him go in there right now and take a moral stand—right now, not later. Tell him, don't wait until election time. If he waits too long, brothers and sisters, he will be responsible for letting a condition develop in this country which will create a climate that will bring seeds up out of the ground with vegetation on the end of them looking like something these people never dreamed of. In 1964, it's the ballot or the bullet. Thank you.

Less than a year after this speech, Malcolm X was murdered. At his funeral, actor Ossie Davis gave the eulogy and called him "our own black shining prince."

AUTHOR

Malcom X (1925–1965), the son of a Baptist preacher, was born Malcolm Little in Omaha, Nebraska. At the age of twenty-one he was sentenced to six years in jail for burglary. While in prison, Malcolm converted to the Nation of Islam, a religion that advocates complete separation from white society. (Members of the Nation of Islam have also been called Black Muslims.) His growing distress over the Nation of Islam's refusal to join in the civil rights movement caused Malcolm to break with the sect. He was assassinated by Black Muslims on February 25, 1965, during a speech in Harlem.

RESPONSE

For many African Americans, especially young people in the northern cities, the speech reinforced their self-respect. Frustrated by what they saw as the slow pace of change brought about through the nonviolent tactics of leaders like Martin Luther King, Jr., they were attracted to the more militant position of Malcolm X. In contrast, many whites were frightened and angered by what they saw as Malcolm X's threat of violence by African Americans. In the summer of 1967 such violence did erupt when African Americans rioted in cities such as Newark, New Jersey, and Detroit, Michigan.

In 1964, after Malcolm X left the Nation of Islam and made a holy pilgrimage to Mecca, he took the Arabic name El-Haji Malik El-Shabazz. However, he is still known to the world as Malcolm X— a controversial figure to some and a hero to many.

Malcolm X was photographed in Egypt on his way to Mecca, the holy city of the Islamic religion. After this trip, Malcolm X softened his belief that African Americans should live separately from white society in the United States.

Speech to Striking Grape Workers

(MARCH 1, 1966)

César Chávez

In another speech César Chávez asked, "How long will it be before we take seriously the importance of the workers who harvest the food we eat?"

This speech is commonly called "God Is Beside You on the Picket Line."

In 1966 Mexican grape workers were striking in California. The goal was to increase public sympathy about the poor working conditions of migrant farm laborers. The grape workers made an average of $.90 per hour. Their average life expectancy in 1966 was forty-nine years. Child labor was common and many laborers were injured or died due to poor working and living conditions. The striking workers demanded rest periods, clean drinking water and hand-washing facilities, and, because they came into contact with chemical pesticides while working, they wanted pesticide spraying banned while laborers were in the fields. Their leader, César Chávez, led a 250-mile Easter march from Delano, California, to the state capital at Sacramento. When the marchers reached the capital, Chávez delivered this short speech. By the end of the 1960s his efforts had helped Mexican Americans to organize politically. They wanted to end discrimination against them and be treated equally, just like other Americans.

In the "March from Delano to Sacramento" there is a meeting of cultures and traditions; the centuries-old religious tradition of Spanish culture conjoins with the very contemporary cultural syndrome of "demonstration" springing from the spontaneity of the poor, the downtrodden, the rejected, the discriminated against bearing visibly their need and demand for equality and freedom.

In every religion-oriented culture "the pilgrimage" has had a place: a trip made with sacrifice and hardship as an expression of penance and of commitment—and often involving a petition to the patron of the pilgrimage for some sincerely sought benefit of body or soul. Pilgrimage has not passed from Mexican culture. Daily at any of the major shrines of the country and in particular at the Basilica of the Lady of Guadalupe, there arrive pilgrims from all points—some of whom may have long since walked out the pieces of rubber tire that once served them as soles, and many of whom will walk on their knees the last mile or so of the pilgrimage. Many of the "pilgrims" of Delano will have walked such pilgrimages themselves in their lives—perhaps as very small children even—and cling to the memory of

During their struggle to unionize, 95 percent of the strikers lost their homes and their cars because they had no work.

This photo, taken in March 1975, shows César Chávez and Mexican-American migrant workers marching and demanding that California grape growers recognize the United Farm Workers Union.

Throughout the 1960s Mexican Americans regarded César Chávez with the same admiration and respect that African Americans felt for Martin Luther King, Jr.

the day-long marches, the camps at night, streams forded, hills climbed, the sacral aura of the sanctuary, and the "fiesta" that followed.

But throughout the Spanish-speaking world there is another tradition that touches the present march, that of the Lenten penitential processions, where the *penitentes* would march through the streets, often in sack cloth and ashes, some even carrying crosses, as a sign of penance for their sins, and as a plea for the mercy of God. The penitential procession is also in the blood of the Mexican American, and the Delano march will therefore be one of penance—public penance for the sins of the strikers, their own personal sins as well as their yielding perhaps to feelings of hatred and revenge in the strike itself. They hope by the march to set themselves at peace with the Lord, so that the justice of their cause will be purified of all lesser motivation.

These two great traditions of a great people meet in the Mexican American with the belief that Delano is his "cause," his great demand for justice, freedom, and respect from a predominantly foreign cultural community in a land where he was first. The revolutions of Mexico were primarily uprisings of the poor, fighting for bread and for dignity. The Mexican-American is also a child of the revolution.

Pilgrimage, penance and revolution. The pilgrimage from Delano to Sacramento has strong religio-cultural overtones. But it is also the pilgrimage of a cultural minority which has suffered from a hostile environment, and a minority which means business.

AUTHOR

César Chávez (1927–1993) was the founder and director of the United Farm Workers Association. He was born in Arizona to immigrant parents. In 1962 he decided to devote all his energies to organizing a union for farmworkers. Chávez used the same tactics as the civil rights movement, such as nonviolence, sit-ins, and marches. The union he founded was the first union of migratory workers in the United States.

RESPONSE

César Chávez began winning nationwide attention for his cause. In 1969 Americans of all ethnicities supported the strikers by joining in a nationwide boycott of California grapes. A year later, the grape growers finally recognized the union.

Influenced by Chávez, other Mexican-American leaders began to work for bilingual educational programs to improve language skills and economic and social opportunities for their people.

This poster advertises a 1968 performance in support of the United Farm Workers Union to be held at New York City's Carnegie Hall. Two years later, after five years of conflict, the growers recognized the union.

The Eagle Has Landed

(JULY 21, 1969)

This picture, taken from the lunar module, shows the astronauts planting the United States flag on the surface of the moon. Neil Armstrong stands on the left, and astronaut Edwin Aldrin, Jr., stands on the right.

About 600 million people around the world watched the moon landing and walk on television. The American flag placed on the moon's surface has this message on it: "We come in peace for all mankind."

In 1961 President John F. Kennedy promised to beat the Soviets in the space race by landing an astronaut on the moon before the decade's end. Eight years later, the lunar module of *Apollo 11* gently touched down near the moon's Sea of Tranquility. Astronaut Neil Armstrong stepped onto the moon's surface, becoming the first human to walk on the moon.

The moon landing was one of the highlights of American space exploration, which continues to the present. The focus of space exploration has changed; now the National Aeronautics and Space Administration (NASA) sends unmanned probes and conducts experiments aboard the space shuttles. The excitement of seeing humans walk on the moon has never been matched, however. This excerpt is from a three-way conversation among Armstrong, his fellow astronaut Edwin "Buzz" Aldrin, Jr., and flight control center in Houston, Texas (identified here as Duke), during the landing.

102:45:43 Armstrong (onboard): Shutdown.

102:45:44 Aldrin: Okay. Engine Stop.

102:45:45 Aldrin: ACA out of Detent.

102:45:46 Armstrong: Out of Detent. Auto. [The control stick was moved away from its centered position.]

102:45:47 Aldrin: Mode Control, both Auto. Descent Engine Command Override, Off. Engine Arm, Off. 413 is in. [413 is computer data that tells that the lunar module has landed.]

102:45:57 Duke: We copy you down, Eagle.

102:45:58 Armstrong (onboard): Engine arm is off. (Pause) Houston, Tranquility Base here. The Eagle has landed.

102:46:06 Duke: Roger, Tranquility. We copy you on the ground. You got a bunch of guys about to turn blue. We're breathing again. Thanks a lot.

102:46:16 Aldrin: Thank you.

102:46:18 Duke: You're looking good here.

As he stepped on the moon, Neil Armstrong said, "That's one small step for man, one giant leap for mankind."

ASTRONAUTS

Neil Armstrong (1930–) was born in Ohio. In 1949 he became a navy pilot. Armstrong joined the astronaut program in 1962 and retired in 1971. He received the Presidential Medal of Freedom in 1969. Edwin (Buzz) Aldrin, Jr., (1930–) was born in New Jersey. During the Korean War he flew combat missions. He was selected as an astronaut in 1963 and retired in 1971. Aldrin received the Exceptional Service Medal for his achievements as an astronaut.

In 1961 the Soviet Union sent the first man into space. Afterward, Americans realized that they needed to catch up to the Soviets. With more money put into the United States space agency (NASA), American astronauts went on a series of space missions, called the Mercury and Gemini projects, to explore space. What NASA learned from these earlier missions paved the way for the Apollo program and the moon landing.

RESPONSE

People around the world praised the moon landing. But in America reaction was mixed. Critics of the space program thought that the enormous amount of money spent on it should have gone into programs that helped society. Meanwhile, some Americans even believed that the moon walk was a fake event, staged to keep the focus of attention off the controversial war in Vietnam.

I'd Rather Be Black Than Female

(1970)

Shirley Chisholm

Chisholm announced her backing of Senator George McGovern after she lost her bid to be the Democratic presidential hopeful.

In 1968 Shirley Chisholm became the first African-American woman elected to the U.S. House of Representatives.

Two years later, in her autobiography, *Unbought and Unbossed*, she described the obstacles she had to overcome to succeed in the political world. She concluded that prejudice against women held her back more than racism. Many feminists felt that Shirley Chisholm was right and that if women wanted to gain more power in American society, they needed to get elected to political office. In the following years, more and more women ran for political office. Twenty-four years after Chisholm's election, the first African-American woman, Carol Moseley-Braun, was elected to the U.S. Senate.

Being the first black woman elected to Congress has made me some kind of phenomenon. There are nine other blacks in Congress; there are ten other women. I was the first to overcome both handicaps at once. Of the two handicaps, being black is much less of a drawback than being female.

If I said that being black is a greater handicap than being a woman, probably no one would question me. Why? Because "we all know" there is prejudice against black people in America. That there is prejudice against women is an idea that still strikes nearly all men—and, I am afraid, most women—as bizarre.

Prejudice against blacks was invisible to most white Americans for many years. When blacks finally started to "mention" it, with sit-ins, boycotts, and freedom rides, Americans were incredulous. "Who, us?" they asked in injured tones. "*We're* prejudiced?" It was the start of a long, painful reeducation for white America. It will take years for whites—including those who think of themselves as liberals—to discover and eliminate the racist attitude they all actually have.

How much harder will it be to eliminate the prejudice against women? I am sure it will be a longer struggle. Part of the problem is that women in America are much more brainwashed and content with their roles as second-class citizens than blacks ever were.

Let me explain. I have been active in politics for more than twenty years. For all but the last six, I have done the work—all the tedious details that make the difference between victory and defeat on election day—while men reaped the rewards, which is almost invariably the lot of women in politics.

It is still women—about three million volunteers—who do most of this work in the American political world. The best any of them can hope for is the honor of being district or county vice chairman, a kind of separate-but-equal position with which a woman is rewarded for years of faithful envelope stuffing and card-party organizing. In such a job, she gets a number of free trips to state and sometimes national meetings and conventions, where her role is supposed to be to vote the way her male chairman votes.

When I tried to break out of that role in 1963 and run for

Shirley Chisholm said about her campaign to be the Democratic presidential nominee, "I began to open the way for women to think they can run."

In 1984 Shirley Chisholm helped start the National Political Congress for Black Women. The new organization's goal was to encourage African-American women to run for political office.

the New York State Assembly seat from Brooklyn's Bedford-Stuyvesant, the resistance was bitter. From the start of that campaign, I faced undisguised hostility because of my sex.

But it was four years later, when I ran for Congress, that the question of my sex became a major issue. Among members of my own party, closed meetings were held to discuss ways of stopping me. . . .

When a bright young woman graduate starts looking for a job, why is the first question always: "Can you type?" A history of prejudice lies behind that question. Why are women thought of as secretaries, not administrators? Librarians and teachers, but not doctors and lawyers? Because they are thought of as different and inferior. The happy homemaker and the contented darky are both stereotypes produced by prejudice.

Women have not even reached the level of tokenism that blacks are reaching. No women sit on the Supreme Court. Only two have held Cabinet rank and none do at present. Only two women hold ambassadorial rank. But women predominate in the lower-paying, menial, unrewarding, dead-end jobs, and when they do reach better positions, they are invariably paid less than a man gets for the same job.

If that is not prejudice, what would you call it?

A few years ago, I was talking with a political leader about a promising young woman as a candidate. "Why invest time and effort to build the girl up?" he asked me. "You know she'll only drop out of the game to have a couple of kids just about the time we're ready to run her for mayor."

Plenty of people have said similar things about me. Plenty of others have advised me, every time I tried to take another upward step, that I should go back to teaching, a woman's vocation, and leave politics to the men. I love teaching, and I am ready to go back to it as soon as I am convinced that this country no longer needs a woman's contribution.

When there are no children going to bed hungry in this rich nation, I may be ready to go back to teaching. When there is a good school for every child, I may be ready. When we do not spend our wealth on hardware to murder people, when we no longer tolerate prejudice against minorities, and when the laws against unfair housing and unfair employment practices are enforced instead of evaded, then there may be nothing more for me to do in politics.

But until that happens—and we all know it will not be this year or next—what we need is more women in politics, because we have a very special contribution to make. I hope that the example of my success will convince other women to get into politics—and not just to stuff envelopes, but to run for office.

It is women who can bring empathy, tolerance, insight, patience, and persistence to government—the qualities we naturally have or have had to develop because of our suppression by men. The women of a nation mold its morals, its religion, and its politics by the lives they live. At present, our country needs women's idealism and determination, perhaps more in politics than anywhere else.

Shirley Chisholm (right) shook hands with people in Boston during her 1972 campaign to become the Democratic candidate for president.

AUTHOR

Shirley Chisholm (1924–) was born in Brooklyn, New York. First a teacher, then a politician, she represented her Brooklyn district in Congress for seven terms, retiring in 1982. While in Congress, she was a strong supporter of civil rights. In 1972 she became the first African American to campaign for the Democratic party nomination for president. On the first nominating ballot, she received more than 150 votes.

RESPONSE

Chisholm's book attracted some attention, mainly among feminists, but American men generally ignored her message. Her writing did, however, inspire younger feminists to run for office and speak out against discrimination.

LETTER OF RESIGNATION

(AUGUST 9, 1974)

RICHARD M. NIXON

President Nixon, seated at his desk, announced his resignation on August 8, 1974. Nixon is the only American president to resign his office—doing so under the threat of impeachment—and accept a pardon for wrongdoings in the Oval Office.

During the Watergate scandal, President Nixon went on television and announced, "I am not a crook."

In late July, the House Judiciary Committee voted to adopt three articles of impeachment against President Richard M. Nixon because of his role in the Watergate scandal. The trouble began in 1972, when Republican campaign officials broke into the Democratic national headquarters located in the Washington, D.C., Watergate apartment house and office building. Although the president seemed to have not known in advance about the crime, he apparently tried to cover it up.

The articles of impeachment charged him with obstructing justice, misusing his powers, violating his oath of office, and refusing to produce material the committee had requested. Realizing that the House would almost certainly vote to impeach, Nixon wrote to Secretary of State Henry Kissinger, resigning the presidency. With this letter, he became the first president to resign. The behavior that led to his leaving in disgrace made the public more mistrustful of politics. An orderly transfer of power occurred as Vice President Gerald Ford assumed the presidency.

Dear Mr. Secretary:

I hereby resign the Office of President of the United States.

Up to the last minute, President Nixon did not want to resign. But Republican leaders in Congress informed him that a majority of senators would vote for his impeachment.

AUTHOR

California-born Richard M. Nixon (1913–1994) was the thirty-seventh president of the United States. Elected vice president in 1952, he served two terms under Republican president Dwight D. Eisenhower. In 1960 Nixon lost the presidential race to Democrat John F. Kennedy but won it in 1968, defeating Vice President Hubert Humphrey. Nixon's major achievements in office were in foreign policy, and one of the high points was the opening of relations between the United States and China. After resigning, he spent the rest of his life rebuilding his reputation.

President Nixon addressed his resignation letter to the secretary of state because he was following a 1792 act of Congress that established procedures for federal officials resigning from office.

RESPONSE

When Gerald Ford was sworn in as president on August 9, 1974, Americans were relieved that the turmoil had ended. The new president himself summed up most of the public's feelings best. Said Ford, "The long nightmare is over." A month later, he granted Nixon a full pardon so that the nation could move on. But the pardon sparked its own controversy. Many Americans did not want a former president in jail even if he was guilty. But others felt that if he was innocent, then it was wrong to pardon him for crimes he had not even been charged with.

This 1973 photo shows Bob Woodward (left) and Carl Bernstein (right), two young reporters for the Washington Post *newspaper. Their investigations of the Watergate case and President Nixon's role in it helped bring Watergate to the attention of the American people.*

Farewell Address

(JANUARY 11, 1989)

Ronald Reagan

This photo of Ronald and Nancy Reagan was taken in November 1981 on the White House grounds. Earlier that year, President Reagan was shot by would-be assassin John Hinckley, Jr. The president recovered quickly, and his strength and humor during the precarious time helped increase his popularity with the American people.

When Ronald Reagan first became president in 1980, he promised Americans an "era of national renewal." He believed that government had become too powerful and complicated, and that it was hurting people more than it was helping them. Throughout his eight years in office, he lowered taxes and slashed funding for social services, eliminating food stamp programs and spending less money on education and health care. He also introduced a new approach to economics (known as "Reaganomics") in an effort to lead America out of its worst recession (in 1982) since World War II. By 1984 the economy was booming—millions of new jobs were created and the stock market was soaring.

Reagan was also determined to win the fight against Communism and the Soviet Union, spending lots of money building up the military and supporting anti-Communist forces in Afghanistan and Nicaragua. He also sent U.S. troops to invade the pro-Communist government in Grenada.

This is the 34th time I'll speak to you from the Oval Office and the last. We've been together 8 years now, and soon it'll be time for me to go. But before I do, I wanted to share some thoughts, some of which I've been saving for a long time.

. . . From Grenada to the Washington and Moscow summits, from the recession of '81 to '82, to the expansion that began in late '82 and continues to this day, we've made a difference. The way I see it, there were two great triumphs, two things that I'm proudest of. One is the economic recovery, in which the people of America created—and filled—19 million new jobs. The other is the recovery of our morale. America is respected again in the world and looked to for leadership.

Something that happened to me a few years ago reflects some of this. It was back in 1981, and I was attending my first big economic summit, which was held that year in Canada. The meeting place rotates among the member countries. The opening meeting was a formal dinner of the heads of government of the seven industrialized nations. Now, I sat there like the new kid in school and listened, and it was all François this and Helmut that. They dropped titles and spoke to one another on a first-name basis. Well, at one point I sort of leaned in and said, 'My name's Ron.' Well, in that same year, we began the actions we felt would ignite an economic comeback—cut taxes and regulation, started to cut spending. And soon the recovery began.

Two years later, another economic summit with pretty much the same cast. At the big opening meeting we all got together, and all of a sudden, just for a moment, I saw that everyone was just sitting there looking at me. And then one of them broke the silence. 'Tell us about the American miracle,' he said.

Well, back in 1980, when I was running for President, it was all so different. Some pundits said our programs would result in catastrophe. Our views on foreign affairs would cause war. Our plans for the economy would cause inflation to soar and bring about economic collapse. I even remember one highly respected economist saying, back in 1982, that 'The engines of economic growth have shut down here, and they're likely to stay that way for years to come.' Well, he and the other opinion leaders were wrong. The fact is what they call 'radical' was

President Reagan visited the Soviet Union for the first time in 1988. He and Mikhail Gorbachev are shown here in Moscow's Red Square. Just a few months earlier, in December 1987, the two leaders signed a treaty that cut the amount of nuclear weapons the two superpowers possessed. This ended the Cold War between the Soviet Union and the United States and was the beginning of glasnost, *or the opening up of Soviet society.*

Ronald Reagan was sixty-nine years old when he was inaugurated, making him the oldest president to be sworn into office. He was seventy-seven when he left office in 1988.

Reagan's nickname was The Great Communicator because he was able to clearly state his key issues. He made complex political and economic issues understandable to the American people.

really 'right.' What they called 'dangerous' was just 'desperately needed.'

And in all of that time I won a nickname, 'The Great Communicator.' But I never though it was my style or the words I used that made a difference: it was the content. I wasn't a great communicator, but I communicated great things, and they didn't spring full bloom from my brow, they came from the heart of a great nation—from our experience, our wisdom, and our belief in the principles that have guided us for two centuries. They called it the Reagan revolution. Well, I'll accept that, but for me it always seemed more like the great rediscovery, a rediscovery of our values and our common sense.

Common sense told us that when you put a big tax on something, the people will produce less of it. So, we cut the people's tax rates, and the people produced more than ever before. The economy bloomed like a plant that had been cut back and could now grow quicker and stronger. Our economic program brought about the longest peacetime expansion in our history: real family income up, the poverty rate down, entrepreneurship booming, and an explosion in research and new technology. We're exporting more than ever because American industry became more competitive and at the same time, we summoned the national will to knock down protectionist walls abroad instead of erecting them at home.

Common sense also told us that to preserve the peace, we'd have to become strong again after years of weakness and confusion. So, we rebuilt our defenses, and this New Year we toasted the new peacefulness around the globe. Not only have the superpowers actually begun to reduce their stockpiles of nuclear weapons—and hope for even more progress is bright—but the regional conflicts that rack the globe are also beginning to cease. The Persian Gulf is no longer a war zone. The Soviets are leaving Afghanistan. The Vietnamese are preparing to pull out of Cambodia, and an American-mediated accord will soon send 50,000 Cuban troops home from Angola.

The lesson of all this was, of course, that because we're a great nation, our challenges seem complex. It will always be this way. But as long as we remember our first principles and believe in ourselves, the future will always be ours. And something else we learned: Once you begin a great movement, there's no telling where it will end. We meant to change a nation, and instead, we changed a world.

. . . Ours was the first revolution in the history of mankind that truly reversed the course of government, and with three little words: 'We the People.' 'We the People' tell the government what to do; it doesn't tell us. 'We the People' are the driver; the government is the car. And we decide where it should go, and by what route, and how fast. Almost all the world's constitutions are documents in which governments tell the people what their privileges are. Our Constitution is a document in which 'We the People' tell the government what it is allowed to do. 'We the People' are free. This belief has been the underlying basis for everything I've tried to do these past 8 years.

. . . Nothing is less free than pure communism—and yet we have, the past few years, forged a satisfying new closeness with the Soviet Union. I've been asked if this isn't a gamble, and my answer is no because we're basing our actions not on words but deeds. The détente of the 1970's was based not on actions but promises. They'd promise to treat their own people and the people of the world better. But the *gulag* was still the *gulag*, and the state was still expansionist, and they still waged proxy wars in Africa, Asia, and Latin America.

Well, this time, so far, it's different. President Gorbachev has brought about some internal democratic reforms and begun the withdrawal from Afghanistan. He has also freed prisoners whose names I've given him every time we've met. . . .

We must keep up our guard, but we must also continue to work together to lessen and eliminate tension and mistrust. My view is that President Gorbachev is different from previous Soviet leaders. I think he knows some of the things wrong with his society and is trying to fix them. We wish him well. And we'll continue to work to make sure that the Soviet Union that eventually emerges from this process is a less threatening one. What it all boils down to is this: I want the new closeness to continue. And it will, as long as we make it clear that we will continue to act in a certain way as long as they continue to act in a helpful manner. If and when they don't, at first pull your punches. If they persist, pull the plug. It's still trust by verify.

When Reagan was reelected in 1984, he won more votes than any previous president.

During his acting years, Ronald Reagan appeared in more than 50 films. One of his most-beloved roles was his portrayal of football player George Gipp in Knute Rockne–All American *(1940).*

In November, 1994, Ronald Reagan was diagnosed with Alzheimer's disease. Since that time, Nancy Reagan has become an outspoken advocate for individuals and families affected by the disease.

It's still play, but cut the cards. It's still watch closely. And don't be afraid to see what you see.

. . . Now, we're about to enter the nineties, and some things have changed. Younger parents aren't sure that an unambivalent appreciation of America is the right thing to teach modern children. And as for those who create the popular culture, well-grounded patriotism is no longer the style. Our spirit is back, but we haven't reinstitutionalized it. We've got to do a better job of getting across that America is freedom—freedom of speech, freedom of religion, freedom of enterprise. And freedom is special and rare. It's fragile; it needs protection.

. . . And let me offer lesson number one about America: All great change in America begins at the dinner table. So, tomorrow night in the kitchen I hope the talking begins. And children, if your parents haven't been teaching you what it means to be an American, let 'em know and nail 'em on it. That would be a very American thing to do.

And that's about all I have to say tonight, except for one thing. The past few days . . . I've thought a bit of the 'shining city upon a hill.' The phrase comes from John Winthrop, who wrote it to describe the America he imagined. What he imagined was important because he was an early Pilgrim, an early freedom man. He journeyed here on what today we'd call a little wooden boat; and like the other Pilgrims, he was looking for a home that would be free. I've spoken of the shining city all my political life, but I don't know if I ever quite communicated what I saw when I said it. But in my mind it was a tall, proud city built on rocks stronger than oceans, windswept, God-blessed, and teeming with people of all kinds living in harmony and peace; a city with free ports that hummed with commerce and creativity. And if there had to be city walls, the walls had doors and the doors were open to anyone with the will and the heart to get here. That's how I saw it, and see it still.

And how stands the city on this winter night? More prosperous, more secure, and happier than it was 8 years ago. But more than that: After 200 years, two centuries, she still stands strong and true on the granite ridge, and her glow has held steady no matter what storm. And she's still a beacon, still a magnet for all who must have freedom, for all the pilgrims from all the lost places who are hurtling through the darkness, toward home.

We've done our part. And as I walk off into the city streets, a final word to the men and women of the Reagan revolution, the men and women across America who for 8 years did the work that brought America back. My friends: We did it. We weren't just marking time. We made a difference. We made the city stronger, we made the city freer, and we left her in good hands. All in all, not bad, not bad at all.

And so, goodbye, God bless you, and God bless the United States of America.

AUTHOR

Ronald Wilson Reagan (1911–) was one of the most popular presidents in U.S. history. Born into a poor Illinois family, Reagan became a radio announcer and then, using his considerable charm and good looks, a Hollywood actor. As president of the Screen Actors Guild, Reagan's energy, wit, speech-making talents, and charisma began to be recognized. He used these skills to be elected Republican governor of California in 1966, and then president in 1980 and then, again, in 1984.

During Reagan's first term in office, relations between the United States and the Soviet Union were anything but friendly. In 1983 Reagan called the Soviet Union an "evil empire." This photo of President Reagan and Soviet leader Mikhail Gorbachev was taken at the 1986 superpower summit in Reykjavik. Relations between the two countries began to improve during this time.

RESPONSE

President Ronald Reagan was a highly appealing personality and a gifted speech-maker. When he spoke, he made a very strong impression. He appeared to be a man of principle and conviction, making Americans feel protected, secure, and proud of their country. This talent served him well throughout his eight years in office. Although the economy exploded during his presidency he left the United States with an enormous national debt. And, although the rich got richer, his domestic policies left many people feeling abandoned.

Finally, the Reagan administration was the center of much controversy, when it was discovered that they had been secretly selling weapons to Iran and funding an anti-Communist war in Nicaragua.

SPEECH AT THE UNITED NATIONS CONFERENCE ON WOMEN

(SEPTEMBER 5, 1995)

HILLARY RODHAM CLINTON

First Lady Hillary Rodham Clinton addressed the U.N. Conference on Women on September 5, 1995.

Hillary Rodham Clinton, the wife of President William Clinton, journeyed to China to address participants at the Fourth World Conference on Women, held in Beijing. Mrs. Clinton was the head of the U.S. delegation. But some Americans, disturbed by China's poor record on human rights, criticized her for participating. In her remarks, Mrs. Clinton strongly supported the rights of women everywhere. People around the world praised the speech for demonstrating American concern with the right of women to lead lives of dignity and equality.

. . . At this very moment, as we sit here, women around the world are giving birth, raising children, cooking meals, washing clothes, cleaning houses, planting crops, working on assembly lines, running companies, and running countries.

Women are also dying from diseases that should have been prevented or treated; they are watching their children succumb to malnutrition caused by poverty and economic deprivation; they are being denied the right to go to school by their own fathers and brothers; they are being forced into prostitution, and they are being barred from the ballot box and the bank-lending office.

Those of us with the opportunity to be here have the responsibility to speak for those who could not.

As an American, I want to speak up for women in my own country—women who are raising children on the minimum wage, women who can't afford health care or child care, women whose lives are threatened by violence, including violence in their own homes.

I want to speak up for mothers who are fighting for good schools, safe neighborhoods, clean air and clean airwaves. . . for older women, some of them widows, who have raised their families and now find that their skills and life experiences are not valued in the workplace. . . for women who are working all night as nurses, hotel clerks, and fast food chefs so that they can be at home during the day with their kids. . . and for women everywhere who simply don't have enough time to do everything they are called upon to do each day.

Speaking to you today, I speak for them, just as each of us speaks for women around the world who are denied the chance to go to school, or see a doctor, or own property, or have a say about the direction of their lives, simply because they are women.

The truth is that most women around the world work both inside and outside the home, usually by necessity.

We need to understand that there is no formula for how women should lead their lives. That is why we must respect the choices that each woman makes for herself and her family. Every woman deserves the chance to realize her God-given potential.

Women from 180 countries attended the conference.

During Mrs. Clinton's speech, her audience showed their approval by thumping desks as well as by applauding.

We must also recognize that women will never gain full dignity until their human rights are respected and protected.

Our goals for this conference, to strengthen families and societies by empowering women to take greater control over their own destinies, cannot be fully achieved unless all governments—here and around the world—accept their responsibility to protect and promote internationally recognized human rights.

The international community has long acknowledged—and recently affirmed at Vienna—that both women and men are entitled to a range of protections and personal freedoms, from the right of personal security to the right to determine freely the number and spacing of the children they bear.

No one should be forced to remain silent for fear of religious or political persecution, arrest, abuse or torture.

Tragically, women are most often the ones whose human rights are violated. Even in the late 20th century, the rape of women continues to be used as an instrument of armed conflict. Women and children make up a large majority of the world's refugees. And when women are excluded from the political process, they become even more vulnerable to abuse.

I believe that, on the eve of a new millennium, it is time to break our silence. It is time for us to say here in Beijing, and the world to hear, that it is no longer acceptable to discuss women's rights as separate from human rights.

These abuses have continued because, for too long, the history of women has been a history of silence. Even today, there are those who are trying to silence our words.

The voices of this conference and of the women at Hairou [Chinese city where women's rights delegates were also meeting] must be heard loud and clear.

It is a violation of *human* rights when babies are denied food, or drowned, or suffocated, or their spines broken, simply because they are girls.

It is a violation of *human* rights when women and girls are sold into the slavery of prostitution.

It is a violation of *human* rights when women are doused with gasoline, set on fire and burned to death because their marriage dowries are deemed too small.

It is a violation of *human* rights when individual women are raped in their own communities and when thousands of women are subjected to rape as a tactic or prize of war.

It is a violation of *human* rights when a leading cause of death worldwide among women ages 14 to 44 is the violence they are subjected to in their own homes.

It is a violation of *human* rights when young girls are brutalized by the painful and degrading practice of genital mutilation.

It is a violation of *human* rights when women are denied the right to plan their own families, and that includes being forced to have abortions or being sterilized against their will.

If there is one message that echoes forth from this conference, it is that human rights are women's rights. . . . And women's rights are human rights.

Let us not forget that among those rights are the right to speak freely. And the right to be heard.

Women must enjoy the right to participate fully in the social and political lives of their countries if we want freedom and democracy to thrive and endure.

It is indefensible that many women in non-governmental organizations who wished to participate in this conference have not been able to attend—or have been prohibited from fully taking part.

Let me be clear. Freedom means the right of people to assemble, organize, and debate openly. It means respecting the views of those who may disagree with the views of their governments. It means not taking citizens away from their loved ones and jailing them, mistreating them, or denying them their freedom or dignity because of the peaceful expression of their ideas and opinions.

In my country, we recently celebrated the 75th anniversary of women's suffrage. It took 150 years after the signing of our Declaration of Independence for women to win the right to vote. It took 72 years of organized struggle on the part of many courageous women and men.

It was one of America's most divisive philosophical wars. But it was also a bloodless war. Suffrage was achieved without a shot fired.

In 1979 the United Nations held the Convention on the Elimination of All Forms of Discrimination against Women. The guidelines put forth at that meeting are often described as a Bill of Rights for women and have now been ratified by 160 countries.

The United Nations' emblem incorporates a map of the globe surrounded by two olive branches, the traditional symbol of peace.

We also have been reminded, in V-J Day observances last weekend, of the good that comes when men and women join together to combat the forces of tyranny and build a better world.

We have seen peace prevail in most places for a half century. We have avoided another world war.

But we have not solved older, deeply rooted problems that continue to diminish the potential of half the world's population.

Now it is time to act on behalf of women everywhere.

If we take bold steps to better the lives of women, we will be taking bold steps to better the lives of children and families too. Families rely on mothers and wives for emotional support and care; families rely on women for labor in the home; and increasingly, families rely on women for income needed to raise healthy children and care for other relatives.

As long as discrimination and inequities remain so commonplace around the world—as long as girls and women are valued less, fed less, fed last, overworked, underpaid, not schooled and subjected to violence in and out of their homes—the potential of the human family to create a peaceful, prosperous world will not be realized.

Let this conference be our—and the world's—call to action.

And let us heed the call so that we can create a world in which every woman is treated with respect and dignity, every boy and girl is loved and cared for equally, and every family has the hope of a strong and stable future.

Thank you very much. God's blessings on you, your work and all who benefit from it.

AUTHOR

Hillary Rodham Clinton (1947–) is a lawyer and the wife of William Clinton, the forty-third president of the United States. Born to a middle-class Illinois family, she met Mr. Clinton when they were both students at law school. After he was elected president in 1992, her husband appointed her to head the Task Force on Health Care Reform. A first lady heading such a reform effort broke precedent, and Hillary Clinton's active role has made her the focus of controversy. She has continued to speak about the rights of women and children, for which she is often praised.

RESPONSE

In 1997, two years after the U.N. Conference on Women, Hillary Rodham Clinton spoke at the United Nations in New York. The occasion was the fiftieth anniversary of the adoption of the U.N.'s Universal Declaration of Human Rights. Referring to the Declaration's first article—which states, "All human beings are born free and equal in dignity and rights. They are endowed with reason and conscience and should act towards one another in a spirit of brotherhood"—Mrs. Clinton said, "Freedom and equality for all depend on whether a citizen truly has a voice." She went on to say, "These rights may be eternal, but so too is the struggle to attain them. Though the darkness of the human heart may recede, it will never go away. It must be with realistic eyes that we look for human rights."

The struggle to respect human rights has defined the history of the United States since 1620. On board the Mayflower, the Pilgrims pledged to make just and equal laws for all passengers. Nearly 400 years later, the United States, and other countries around the world, are still striving to live up to the basic principles of human freedom and dignity.

Women of all nations attended the U.N. Conference on Women. Shown here are delegates from various countries.

AFTERWORD

Part of what makes America so exceptional is its ongoing effort to include the many voices that call it home. Although the documents presented in this book have helped make America great, they are limited in number and so necessarily limited in perspective. This collection represents only the most major political and social initiatives in our history. It does not, however, give complete insight into the heart and home of all of the American people.

Various teachers and librarians were consulted in the effort to make this book both reflective of and complementary to school curricula. But these documents are meant only to serve as touchstones for your knowledge of American history. While this book hopes to capture the spirit of American individuality, ingenuity, and independence, it provides only a taste of the American character. From here, you can explore the complexities of the issues these words raise. A good place to start is on the Internet, where many sites provide access to some of this country's most pivotal documents and speeches.

To read documents in their original form, such as Elizabeth Cady Stanton's draft of *The Woman's Bible* (1895), and to see original paintings and letters, including Alexander Graham Bell's design sketch of a telephone (1876), check out the American Memory Project:

http://memory.loc.gov/ammem/mcchtml/corhom.html
(Library of Congress)

For more documents, including the most famous speeches in American history:

http://douglass.speech.nwu.edu
(Douglass Archives of American Public Address)

Longman, an instructional publishing company, has created a comprehensive American history site as well:

http://longman.awl.com/history
(Addison Wesley Longman)

Because of the diversity of America's history, its present and its future, it is important to recognize the limitations of just one book. We hope this book will encourage you to keep your eyes, ears, and minds open to all of the people who spoke, wrote, and dreamed the words that built this nation.

INDEX

Note: Page numbers in **boldface** *indicate main topics. Those in italics indicate illustration captions.*

A

abolitionists, 62, 65, 73, *76*
Adams, Abigail, *16*, **16-17**
Adams, John, 16-17, *17*, 18, 23, 31
Adams, John Quincy, 17, 58
Addams, Jane, 2, **88-91**, *88*, 91
African Americans
  Black Power, 138-42
  citizenship and male voting rights, 76-81, *80*
  Emancipation Proclamation, 70-73
  first members of Congress, *81*
  first woman elected to Congress, *150*, 150-153
  March on Washington, *132*, 132-37
  school desegregation, 110-13
  See also slavery
Alcatraz occupation, *120*
Aldrin, Edwin, Jr., 148, *148*, 149
almanacs, 6-7
American Colonization Society, 55
Anthony, Susan B., *64*, 100, 101
Antietam, Battle of (1863), 70
Apollo 11, 148
Armstrong, Neil, 148, *148*, 149
atom bomb, 109
Austin, Warren, *109*

B

Baez, Joan, 134
Ballot or the Bullet (1964), **138-43**
Barkley, Alben, *109*
Bates, Daisy, *113*
Bell Ringers Association, 1
Berlin Wall speech (1963), 2-3, **128-31**
Bernstein, Carl, *155*
Big Foot, *86*
bilingual education, 147
Bill of Rights (1789), 11, **39-43**, *41*
Bill of Rights for women (1979), 165
Black Elk, 87
Black Muslims, 143
Black Power movement, 138-42, *140*
Bradford, William, 5
Brown, Minnie Jean, *113*
Brown, Oliver, *110*, 111
Brown v. *Board of Education of Topeka* (1954), **110-13**

C

California, 2, 144-47, 161
California, USS, sinking of, *108*
Capone, Al, 93
Carson, Rachel, **124-27**, *124*
Catt, Carrie Chapman, *100*, 101
Central High School (Little Rock), *112*, *113*
Chavez, César, 2, **144-47**, *144*
Chief Joseph. *See* Joseph, Chief
China, 3, 155, 162
Chisholm, Shirley, **150-53**, *150*, *153*
citizenship, 70, 76, 77, *103*
Civil Rights Act (1964), 137
civil rights movement, 81, 132-37, 138-143
Civil War, 72, *75*
  African-American troops, 72, *78*
  Emancipation Proclamation, 70-73
  Gettysburg Address, 74-75
  income tax, 92
  Uncle Tom's Cabin, 66, 69
Clemenceau, Georges, *95*, 99
Clinton, Hillary Rodham, 3, **162-67**, *162*
Clinton, William, 166
Cold War, 119, 128-31, 156, *157*
Common Sense (1776), *12*, **12-15**
Concord, Battle of, *13*
Congress
  constitutional powers, 26-32, 34, 38, 43, 78
  first African-American members, *81*
  first African-American woman member, 150-153
  income tax powers, 93
  Indian tribe terminations, 120
  Nixon impeachment, 155
  respresentation apportionment, 77
  Congress of Racial Equality, 138, 139
Connally, Tom, *109*
Constitution (1787), **24-43**, *25*, *27*
  Bill of Rights, 11, 39-43, *41*
  ratification, *29*, 38, *38*, *39*, 43
  See also specific amendments
Constitutional Convention (1787), 11, *33*, 42
Continental Congress, First, 11, 16
Continental Congress, Second, 11, 18, 19, 23, *24*
CORE, 138, 139
Cuba, 131
Currier and Ives, *81*

D

Davis, Jefferson, *81*
Davis, Ossie, 142
"day that will live in infamy," 107, 108
DDT (pesticide), 124, 126, 127, *127*
Declaration of Independence (1776), 2, **18-23**, *20*, 60
Declaration of Indian Purpose (1961), 2, **120-23**
Declaration of Sentiments (1848), 2, **60-65**
Douglas, William O., 113
Douglass, Frederick, 71, *76*, 79
Du Bois, W. E. B., 80
Dunlap, John, *20*

E

Eagle Has Landed (1969), **148-49**
Eckford, Elizabeth, *112*, *113*
Eighth Amendment (1789), 42
Eisenhower, Dwight D., *112*, 113, *114*, 155
Ellis Island, *102*, 103
Emancipation Proclamation, **70-73**, 133
"entangling alliances," 44, 48-49, 50
environmental pollution, 124-27
Environmental Protection Agency, 127
Equal Rights Amendment, 101
Equal Rights Party, 100
Everett, Edward, *74*

F

Farewell Address (1796), **44-51**
Farewell Address (1989), **156-61**
Federalist Papers, *35*
Feminists. *See* Women's rights
Fifteenth Amendment (1870), 2, **80-81**
Fifth Amendment (1789), 40
First Amendment (1789), 39
Ford, Gerald, 154, 155
foreign relations
  Monroe Doctrine, 56-59
  Nixon's China policy, 155
  Washington's "entangling

alliances," 44, 48-49, 50
Wilson's Fourteen Points, 94-99
Fort McHenry, 52, 53, 55, *55*
Fourteen Points (1918), **94-99**
Fourteenth Amendment (1868), **76-79**, 111, 113
Fourth Amendment (1789), 40
Franklin, Benjamin, **6-7**, *6*, *7*, 14, 18, *18*, 36, 42
Franklin, James, 6
Freedmen's Bureau, 77, 79
Fugitive Slave Act (1850), 69

G

gangsters, 93, *93*
George III, King, 21
Germany, 94, 99, 128-31
Gettysburg, Battle of (1863), 74, *75*
Gettysburg Address (1863), **74-75**, 115
Ghost Dance, 84, 85, *86*, 87
Glass, Carter, *109*
"God is Beside You on the Picket Line," 144
Gorbachev, Mikhail, *157*, *161*
Gore, Al, 127
Great Britain, 52, *59*, 94, *95*, 128
(*see also* Revolutionary War)
Great Communicator, 158
"Great Rule," 50
Great Society, 131
Grenada invasion, 156

H

Hamilton, Alexander, *35*, *39*, 42, 51
Hancock, John, 23
Harpers Weekly, 75, *80*
Henry, Patrick, 8-11, *8*, *9*
Hinckley, John, Jr., *156*
Hine, Lewis Wickes, *102*
House of Representatives, 26-27, 34, 43
Hull-House (Chicago), 88-91, *88*, *90*, *91*
Humphrey, Hubert, 155
Huske, John, *10*

I

"Ich bin ein Berliner," 128, *129*
"I'd Rather Be Black Than Female" (1970), **150-53**
"I Have a Dream," 2, 132-37
immigrants, *102*, *105*
nativist restrictions, 2, 102-5, *104*
settlement houses, 88, 89-91
Immigration Act (1924), **102-5**
Immigration Act (1965), 105
impeachment process, 35, 154, 155
Inaugural Address (1961), **114-19**
income tax, 92-93, *93*
Independence Hall, 24, *24*
Indian Territory (Oklahoma), 83
Internal Revenue Bureau, 92
Iran-Contra arms sales, 161
"I will fight no more forever" (1877), **82-83**

J

Jackson, Andrew, *54*
Jamestown colony, *5*
Japan, 106-9
Jay, John, *35*
Jefferson, Thomas, 18, *18*, *22*, 23 31, 42, 49
Johnson, Andrew, 77, 79
Johnson, Lyndon B., 131, 142
Joseph, Chief, **82-83**, *82*
judicial power, 36

K

Kennedy, John F., *114*, *116*, *119*, *128*, *134*, 155
Berlin Wall speech, 2-3, **128-31**, *129*, *131*
Inaugural Address, **114-19**
pesticide study, 124, 126
space program, 148
Key, Francis Scott, 52-55, *52*
King, Martin Luther, Jr., 2, 80, **132-37**, *132*, *134*, *137*, 143, 146
Kissinger, Henry, 154
Knute Rockne—All American (film), 160

L

Latin America, 56, 58, 59
League of Nations, 94, *98*, 99
League of Women Voters, 101
Lee, Henry, 48
Letter of Resignation (1974), **154-55**
Letter to John Adams, **16-17**
"liberty or death" speech, 8-11
Liberty Tree, *10*
Lincoln, Abraham, *70*
Emancipation Proclamation, **70-73**, *73*
Gettysburg Address, **74-75**, *74*, 115
income tax refund, *92*
Uncle Tom's Cabin, 69, *69*
Lincoln Memorial, 132, 133
Lindsay, John, 126
Linn, Stanley R., *88*
Little Rock Central High School (Ark.), *112*, *113*
Lloyd George, David, *95*
Lodge, Henry Cabot, 99
Lomax, Louis, 139, 140, 141
Louisiana Purchase, *56*

M

Madison, James
Bill of Rights, 11, 24, *40*, 42
Constitution, 28, 32, 42
Federalist Papers, *35*
Washington's Farewell Address, 51
Malcolm X, **138-43**, *138*, *143*
March on Washington Address (1963), **132-37**, *132*
Marshall, Thurgood, 110, *113*
Massachusetts, 4-5, *13*, 16-17
Mayflower Compact (1620), 1, **4-5**, *4*, 167
McCormack, John, *109*
McGovern, George, 150
McKinley, William, *119*
McNary, Charles, *109*
Mecca, 141, *143*
Mexican-American migrant workers, 2, 144-47, *145*
Mexico, 58
Minutemen, *13*
Monroe, James, **56-59**, *56*
Monroe Doctrine (1823), **56-59**, *59*
moon landing, 148-49, *148*
Moseley-Braun, Carol, 150
Mott, Lucretia, 60, 65
Mount Vernon, *45*
movies, 160

N

NAACP, 80, 110, *113*
National Aeronautics and Space Administration (NASA), 148, 149
National American Woman Suffrage Association, 100, *100*
national anthem, *52*, 52-55
National Archives, 25
National Political Congress for Black Women, 152
National Women's Party, 101
Nation of Islam, 143
Native Americans
Chief Joseph's speech, 82-83
Declaration of Indian Purpose, 120-23
Wounded Knee, 84-87
New Frontier, 119
New Jersey, *16*, 17, *96*
New Orleans, Battle of (1815), *54*
New York, *35*, 60-65, 102, *105*
New York City, *29*, *39*, 46, 103
New Yorker, The 126
Nez Percé Indians, 82-83
Nineteenth Amendment (1920), 2, 16, 65, **100-101**
Ninth Amendment (1789), 42
Nixon, Richard, 2, 119, **154-55**, *154*
Nobel Peace Prize, 91
nonviolence, 137, 143

O

Orlando, Vittorio, *95*
Oswald, Lee Harvey, 119

P

Paine, Thomas, 12-15, *14*
pardon, presidential, 155
Paris, Treaty of (1783), 23
Paris Peace Conference (1919), *95*
Patillo, Melva, *113*
Peace Corps, 119
Pearl Harbor attack (1941), 106-9, *106*, *108*
pesticides, 124-27, *127*
Pilgrims, 4-5, *4*, 167
Plessy v. *Ferguson* (1896), 111, 113
Plymouth colony, 4, 5
political parties, 44, 47, 49, 51
Poor People's Campaign, 137
Poor Richard's Almanack (1733-1758), *6*, **6-7**
Presidency
  Chisholm bid, 150, 151, 153
  constitutional provisions, 33-35, 77
  first woman candidate, 100
  income tax exemption, *92*
  Nixon resignation letter, 154-55
  official homes, 46
  oldest sworn in, 157
  youngest to hold office, *119*
press freedom, 39
Princeton University, *96*, 99
proverbs, 7

R

race riots, 143
Randolph, A. Philip, 80
Ray, Gloria, *113*
Reagan, Nancy, 156, 160
Reagan, Ronald, **156-61**, *156*, *157*, *161*
Reaganomics, 156
Red Cloud, Chief, **84-87**, *84*
Revels, Hiram, *81*
Revere, Paul, 1, 3, *10*
Revolutionary War
  Declaration of Independence, 18-23
  first battle, *13*
  Henry's rallying speech, 8-11
  Paine's pamphlet, 12-15
Rights
  African-American, 80-81, 110-13, 132-37, 138-43
  constitutional protection of, 25, 30-43
  enforcement responsibility, 78
  inalienable, 18, 19
  Mexican-American, 144-47
  Native-American, 120-23
  See also women's rights
Riis, Jacob, *91*
Roosevelt, Franklin D., (1941), **106-9**, *109*
Roosevelt, Theodore, *119*

S

Saunders, Richard (pseud.), 6, 7
school desegregation, 110-13
Sea Around Us, The (1951), 125
Second Amendment (1789), 39
Second Virginia Convention (1775), **8-11**, *9*
Senate, 27-28, 150
Seneca Falls Convention (1848), **60-65**
"separate but equal," 111, 113
settlement houses, 88-91
Seventh Amendment (1789), 42
Seward, William, 70
sexism, 150-53
Silent Spring (1962), **124-27**
Sioux Indians, 84-87
Sixteenth Amendment (1913), **92-93**
Sixth Amendment (1789), 40
slavery, 21, 55
  abolitionists, 62, 65, 73, *76*
  Emancipation Proclamation, 70-73, *72*
  Uncle Tom's Cabin, 2, 66-69
Smith, John, *5*
Smithsonian Institution, 53
Soviet Union, 119, 128-31, 149, 156, *157*, *161*
space program, 148-49
Speech to Striking Grape Workers (1966), **144-47**
Stamp Act (1765), 8, *9*, *10*
Stanton, Elizabeth Cady, 60, *60*, *63*, *64*, 65
Starr, Ellen, 88, 90
"Star-Spangled Banner, The" (1814), **52-55**
Statement on Causes of Wounded Knee (1890), **84-87**
Stowe, Harriet Beecher, 2, **66-69**, *66*
Sullivan, James, 17
Supreme Court, 110-13, *113*, 120

T

taxation, 12, 92-93
Tenth Amendment (1789), 42
Third Amendment (1789), 40
Thomas, Jefferson, *113*
Thomson, Charles, 23
treason, 8, 18, 36
Twenty-seventh Amendment (1992), 43
Twenty Years at Hull-House (1910), **88-91**
Tyler, John, 58

U

Unbought and Unbossed (Chisholm), 150
Uncle Tom's Cabin (1852), 2, *66*, **66-69**, *69*
United Farm Workers, *145*, 147
United Nations Conference on Women (1995), 3, **162-67**, *167*
Universal Declaration of Human Rights (1947), 167

V

Versailles, Treaty of (1919), 99
Vice Presidency, 33, 34, 77
Vietnam War, 131, 137, 149
Virginia, *5*, 8-11, 43, *45*
voting rights. *See* African Americans; Woman suffrage
Voting Rights Act of 1965, 80

W

Walls, Carlotta, 113
War Message to Congress (1941), **106-9**
War of 1812, 52, *54*
Warren, Earl, 112, 113
Washington, George, 27, *33*, *39*, 42, *44*, **44-51**, *50*
Washington, Martha, *51*
Washington Post, *155*
Watergate scandal, 154, *155*
"We come in peace for all mankind," 148
"We Shall Overcome" (song), 134
White, Peregrine, 4
White House, 100, *101*, *116*
Wilson, Woodrow, **94-99**, *94*, *95*, *98*, *101*
Winthrop, John, *5*
woman suffrage, 2, 16, *16*, 17
  Fifteenth Amendment denying, 60, *64*, 81
  movement for, 60, *64*, 65, 100, 101
  Nineteenth Amendment granting, 2, 16, 64, 100-101
women's rights
  Abigail Adams letter, 16-17
  Chisholm on sexism vs. racism, 150-53
  Declaration of Sentiments, 60-65
  traditional denial of, 5, 17, 60, 100
  UN Conference, 162-67
Woodhull, Victoria, 100
Woodward, Bob, *155*
World Anti-slavery Convention, 65
World War I, 50, 94-99
World War II, 106-9
Wounded Knee, Battle of (1890), 82, 84-87, *87*
Wounded Knee takeover (1973), *123*
Wovoka, 84